HOW TO BE ADMIRED & RESPECTED

From Attracting Friends to Persuading Interviewers, We Show You How to Influence Anyone

A. RAJA

Published by Academic Underdogs

Printed in the United Kingdom

First Printing, 2019

ISBN 978-0-9933488-4-6

Academic Underdogs Ltd
Roberts House, 2 Manor Rd, Ruislip, Middlesex HA4 7LB

www.AcademicUnderdogs.com

Contents

Verbal & Body Language Secrets

GRUJEMS

Online Charisma

Charisma Project

Preface

"Tell me about yourself"

This was the first question I received during an interview for the first 'real' job I applied for. It's a simple question, and one that few people should have an issue answering. But as I pondered my answer I realised how little I had to say and how uninteresting my life was.

"My name's Anshul. I'm studying Chemical Engineering at UCL and am on track for a second class honours. I work part-time for a party promotion company and have a bronze Duke of Edinburgh award."

My answer was pretty uninspiring, to say the least. I had worked hard and I had a pretty good CV, but it didn't exactly make for entertaining reading. To the interviewer in front of me, it was probably a carbon copy of every other answer he'd heard that day.

After that interview I vowed to have something powerful to say to the next person who asked me that question. I wanted to be unique, confident and proud—to explain who I was and what I had accomplished with my head held high. I wanted to tell a story.

By finding mentors, learning more about myself, experimenting with ideas (including several crazy ones!) and taking risks, I now have a story I'm proud of. One that keeps getting better and better.

So, let me ask you: *tell me about yourself...*

If you have something interesting and powerful to say, great! You probably don't need this book as you're not the target audience—feel free to close the preview screen on Amazon, or put the book back on the shelf.

If you're struggling to answer this question, then you're in luck. The Level Up series is here to help you, to make sure you have a statement worth making and a life worth living.

Chapter 1
Who am I?

You know those skinny Indian kids who look like they're too young to have a moustache? That was me in high school. It wouldn't have mattered if I was a straight-A student. I would have endured a few crappy years in high school and then had an awesome career filled with fame, fortune and all the trimmings. But, unfortunately, I wasn't very academic either.

After I shaved my 'tash' and got a decent haircut, my social life changed for the better and I made some awesome friends outside of school. I even started to attract attention from the opposite sex. It was a game changer for me. Every time I spoke to girls at school, my cheeks turned red and I sounded like Hodor from Game of Thrones. However, these new girls didn't treat me like the girls at school and as a result, I stopped being shy. One of them eventually became my first girlfriend and my social confidence finally normalised.

At college, I made friends from day one and had no issues meeting new people. There was still a stain of social anxiety leftover from high school but it never really concerned me. My priorities had shifted from not being a social pariah to not being an academic failure. Good grades were all I needed to move onto the next stage in life, so the majority of my time was spent studying or preparing for exams. Study skills were all that mattered and 'social skills' weren't even in the picture. Only at university did I realise how much I had neglected these skills and how crucial they were to the rest of my life.

Prior to university I had been in my comfort zone when it came to making friends. It wasn't a conscious decision but I mainly hung around other Asian males because it was easier— we grew up in the same culture, had similar parents, siblings, interests, etc.,

My first day at university dragged me out of that comfort zone. The guy who sat on my right was an ex-military man from Nigeria; the girl on my left was from the Middle East. Making friends took a little more effort and time than I was used to.

The Revelation

The social anxiety I left behind in high school came roaring back when I started applying for jobs. This is when the cracks really started to show. No matter how much I prepared for interviews, I couldn't handle the pressure and failed to project my true personality. I couldn't relate to 50-year-old managing directors and didn't have the ability to influence them in any way. It's only at this point did I really start looking objectively at my social skills, my 'charisma skills' or 'c-skills', as I like to call them.

Only after reading a few books like 'How to Win Friends & Influence People' and speaking to mentors, did I realise that the problem was bigger than I initially thought. My c-skills, or lack thereof, were effecting various other aspects of my life, including performance in my part-time job, confidence with girls, and relationships with family. People would cut me off when I spoke, my jokes wouldn't come off the way I wanted them to and I was all too familiar with awkward silences. I wasn't socially inept, but after observing my peers I knew I could be so much better.

The Turning Point

This nervous, mumbling, fumbling personality that I left behind in high school was on its way back and I had to stop it. During my second year at university, I made a personal oath to become a charismatic, confident person who could command a room with an engaging story or win over a serious interviewer with a tasteful, well-timed joke. As with any major personal improvement, proactive measures had to be taken. Over the course of 6 months, I adopted good 'social habits' and experimented with a number of techniques to help me improve. It became an obsession of mine that is still very much alive today.

By the end of university I had secured several internship and graduate offers at top firms in the city. This was partly down to my approach to the graduate job race but largely because of the steps I'd taken to reduce my social anxiety and influence senior management. Towards the end of university and the start of my first job, there was a very noticeable change in the way people treated me—not only my colleagues but also friends and dates.

Who am I?

Friends and family I hadn't seen since before university commented on how I'd changed and 'come out of my shell'. I had undoubtedly left university more charismatic than when I started and the steps I took worked for me.

As business owner I rely on my ability to influence others every day, from selling to clients to handling various stake holders. I'm surrounded by some very emotionally intelligent friends and mentors, some of whom have used their c-skills to reach incredible heights in their careers from a young age. You'll get to know some of them over the course of this book. They have all helped me develop How to be Admired & Respected into one of the most effective and comprehensive guides on this topic.

My approach has helped countless 16-25 year olds improve their self-confidence when it comes to building new relationships. The question is, will my approach work for you?

Chapter 2
Who I Think You Are

Unfortunately, the words “charm” and “charisma” are not typically associated with girls in our society, even though they are just as charming and charismatic as men.

A number of women, some of whom I’ve consulted while writing this book, have used their relationship-building skills to elevate themselves both personally and professionally. Some of the most engaging, intelligent and professional people I’ve met have been women and I think it’s a crying shame that we reserve words related to personality, professionalism and charisma for men, and words relating to looks for women.

There is a good chance that you’re a guy, and there may be times in this book when it seems like I’m addressing only you. However, these concepts can also be used by women and if it ever comes across as a male-only book it’s only because, as a man myself, I may be speaking from my experience and my perspective.

Many of the concepts covered, particularly those concerning reducing social anxiety, will help both guys and girls. So, if you are a girl, please don’t be put off by the title of this book or any of the early anecdotes. You will discover many golden nuggets and techniques that can help you realise your ambitions.

My guess is that you are soon to start your first year or are currently attending an institution of higher education. Either way, you want people to like you. Let's face it—all of us do, right? We all care about our social status to some degree and this is wired deep in our psychology. Anyone who says they don't care what people think about them is probably lying.

As with school and college, social hierarchies can form at university. Most of us, either consciously or unconsciously, want to be near the top of the pyramid or at least to avoid being at the bottom. This hierarchy forms in every social network whether we like it or not. It's not as prominent as it is in the animal kingdom, where you could clearly identify the alpha female or male. However, despite our intelligence we are in a perpetual popularity contest with almost everyone around us. It's up to us to either resent this subtle competition and pretend it doesn't exist, or to accept it, embrace it, and become better players. I chose the latter and I hope you do too.

Not every relationship you have is a competition or a game that you need to win. When you're catching up with a few close friends over coffee, there is absolutely no reason to check your body language or be too selective with your words. This is an example of a **low-stakes** situation.

Most of this book is about performing when the stakes are high. For example, in a graduate job interview or when negotiating a coursework extension with your lecturer—scenarios where you need to persuade or influence someone. I will refer to these as **high-stakes** situations throughout this book.

Chapter 3
Who this Book is Definitely for

With study skills, it's much easier to identify who will benefit from my advice because they are easy to measure. I know for sure that anyone who achieved less than 120 UCAS points will find value in my other book, How to ACE Your Degree. However, c-skills are difficult to measure because it's hard to determine what other people truly think of us. If only we could read minds! There are some qualitative ways to measure your c-skills and we will cover those later in the book, but for now there is a very simple way to determine whether this book is **definitely** for you…

"Shy."

Have you ever been associated with or called this word? It's a word that has a negative connotation and is synonymous with being quiet, insecure and unconfident. I used to be called this all the time pre-uni and I absolutely hated it. For a long time, I let this word define who I was and I believed that I couldn't change or control the way I was perceived by others. Boy I was wrong!

Who this Book is Definitely for

Once in a blue moon I am still called 'shy'. However, the difference is that I don't let this word define who I am as much as I did pre-uni. If I want to keep to myself and not be the centre of attention at a social event, it's a choice not a result of social anxiety. I know that, when the stakes are high, I have the ability to perform in any situation with people of various ages and backgrounds. Getting to this stage first required accepting that I was shy and then deciding that I no longer wanted to be burdened by social anxiety.

If you're not shy and feel comfortable socially, this book will still help you become better and give you an edge in the highly competitive graduate job race. If you are a shy or quiet person, first ask yourself: is it a choice or a burden? If it's the latter, this book is definitely for you and will inspire you to make changes that will have a positive effect on many different aspects of your life.

Chapter 4
Who this Book isn't for

Lone lambs. These are highly introverted and socially aloof individuals who seem very content on their own. Typically, lone lambs are intelligent and very cynical about personal relationships. They don't really see the value in having friends and prioritise work or other areas of their lives. Quite often, lone lambs stay away from career paths that involve collaborating with or selling to other people. If you are a lone lamb, I'm surprised that you haven't thrown this book into your recycling bin by now because both you and I know this isn't for you.

Make no mistake, I have nothing against lone lambs. In fact, I know some who are brilliant in their respective fields of study and industries. However, I don't want to waste anyone's time here. At no point will I try to convince you that being socially and emotionally intelligent is worthwhile. This book is for those who want to become more charismatic and influential, and want to know how to get there quickly.

This book is also not for those who are ultra-sceptical and cannot take small leaps of faith. Being a sceptic is good, but you will initially need to trust some of the ideas that I show you regardless of how bizarre they may seem.

Who this Book isn't for

Before you throw the book away on the belief that you are a lone lamb and don't need my help, pause for a moment and ask yourself if you're being honest. Social anxiety and shyness is rarely something we want to admit to because it's seen as a negative trait. Everyone has a degree of self-respect and self-preservation that stops themselves from admitting their faults, and in such cases it's easy to pretend that you're not shy or social awkward and you just choose to be alone, or that you avoid social gatherings because you're working on something more important and not because you're anxious.

To truly change, you need to accept and embrace your faults, not hide from them and pretend they don't exist.

Chapter 5
Nature or Nurture?

We all know at least one person who is admired and respected by most people around them. For me it was Iona. She was one of my friends growing up and was very socially confident. As you'll learn later in this book, achieving a balance between being liked and respected is difficult. However, Iona seemed to be a natural at it. She was the first to throw her name into the hat for Head Girl and was subsequently awarded the title. She wasn't everyone's cup of tea but was widely respected for consistently speaking her mind whilst also being kind to others. How did she come to develop this charisma? We're not taught it at school. How did she find her personality and how did I form mine? Why were we so different? Was it nature or nurture?

When you look at each of our backgrounds, the answers to these questions become pretty clear. Iona had two older sisters and her parents were lawyers. My parents were uneducated but hard-working immigrants from Uganda. In both our family homes, when we walked through the front door after school, there were two options: Either we went into the kitchen or the living room. In my house, family members were usually in the living room watching TV. In her house, her family were often in the kitchen chatting about each other's day. Every evening since she was a little girl, Iona went to the kitchen to join the conversation while I went to watch TV in silence or play video games in my room. This was one of thousands of early influences that shaped her into being an extroverted personality and me into an introverted personality.

As we grew up, each of our introverted and extroverted personalities continuously influenced the choices we made. For example, she chose subjects like English and German while I went for Maths and Sciences. She worked in customer service at Debenhams, while I opted for a paper-round and the backroom at a pharmacy. Our early experiences and influences shaped our personalities and defined our comfort zones. We both remained in our comfort zones because neither of us saw a reason to step out, at least not until university.

When faced with internships and graduate job interviews, we were forced into uncomfortable situations because employers want well-rounded candidates. They look for people who can learn quickly and solve problems while also being able to communicate and build a rapport with others.

The point is, neither personality type is the ‘right’ one to have. Whether you relate to Iona or myself, your goal at university should be to become a well-rounded person by improving both sets of skills together. With regards to c-skills, stepping out of your comfort zone by trying new ideas is the only way to achieve this. My charisma project at the end of this book will help you do just that.

Given that we are already a quarter of our way through our lives, the question is, can we still improve? Do we have to change our personalities? Can you still learn to be admired and respected?

Chapter 6
Is it too Late?

"I'm 20 years old now, nothing's going to change"

"I'm almost 30, I am who I am"

These two comments were made 7 years apart by one of my friends and mentees. At 20, he was a nervous undergrad who nodded his head five times a second. Seven years later he was walking on stage in front of 1000 people to collect the 'Top Salesperson of the Year' award from the managing director of the FTSE100 firm he was working for. He is now CEO of an app development and technology company that he founded.

I don't blame him or anyone else for believing that we can't change because these changes happen very slowly over time and it can be hard to notice them. However, from this example, and by observing others over time, it's clear to see that our ability to influence others and self-confidence can improve. Our personalities are somewhat malleable, but there is, of course, a time limit.

At birth our brain is like a sponge that soaks in the world through our parents or guardians. As time goes by this sponge solidifies and by the time we hit 35 years old, we are more or less the person we are going to be for the rest of our lives. It is possible to improve and become more charismatic beyond this age, but it's much harder to do so.

At university, you are still very much still a sponge. You may not feel like it, but you are. Ask anyone 10 years older than you if they are the same person they were 10 years ago and I guarantee they'll say no. Depending on your influences and how much you push yourself, you can mould yourself into an incredibly skilled individual who can sell yourself and your ideas to anyone. It is not too late to do so, in fact, university is the perfect time to make these changes!

Chapter 7
Why Now is the Perfect Time to Experiment

At school or college, you may have consciously or unconsciously felt the need to be 'socially consistent'. For example, if you had a reputation for being a bit of a joker in class, and one day started to be serious about a topic, someone would probably notice the change and might even call you out on it. The same might happen if you were known for being reserved or quiet and decided to be more vocal. Everyone knows you as the person you have portrayed yourself to be and they expect you to continue to be that person.

Doing or saying anything that is not consistent with that reputation will feel very uncomfortable. It's easy to become a prisoner to your own reputation as a kid when you haven't developed the inner confidence and strength to project your personality regardless of the judgement of others.

In year 8, I built a reputation for being shy. After realising where I was going wrong, it was too late and my reputation had stuck. In year 10, I was a much more confident and socially aware person, but I felt this subtle pressure from everyone around me to be consistent. This came in the form of sniggers, giggles, facial expressions and comments like these…

"Look who's piping up?"

"It's always the quiet ones, ay?"

"I didn't know he could talk."

These comments would feel like pin pricks if they were said now, but back then they felt like baseball bats to the head. Whenever the teacher asked a question that I knew the answer to, I'd think twice before answering out of fear of being humiliated in front of the class. Even when people stopped making these comments in year 11, I still was reluctant to put my hand up even though the rational part of my brain knew nothing would happen.

All of this is very similar to negative reinforcement used to train animals. When your dog defecates on your carpet, what are you supposed to do? Most owners punish the dog by putting them in isolation or doing a 'scruff shake'. After several incidents and punishments, the dog associates defecating on the carpet with some form of negative outcome. In the same way, negative or hurtful comments directed towards you can train you into behaving a certain way, and this happens slowly and unconsciously over time. Fortunately, every time you form a new social network with new friends and peers, it creates an opportunity to break free from previous moulds and to develop as an individual.

Luckily for you, at university people are much more forgiving because they have reached a certain level of maturity. This provides the perfect environment to experiment with new ideas and re-invent yourself

Chapter 8
What does Charisma Look Like?

Barack Obama, Jennifer Lawrence, Russell Brand and Cardi B. These are all widely different people who are, by my definition, admired and respected. To understand what charisma is, looking at people in the public eye is a good place to start. Being successful in most industries requires a high level of emotional intelligence and good c-skills. This is specifically true in the entertainment industry and politics.

Politicians in particular are worth studying because they can help us differentiate between good and bad charisma. Elections are essentially nationwide popularity contests. Countless studies have shown that most people vote for the politicians based on personal opinions rather than the policies that they promote. When the likes of Barack Obama or Nick Clegg made large strides in their career and won for their party, I paid close attention and asked questions like…

What parts of their personalities do people like?

What verbal and body language do they use?

How do they project their voice?

What do they say a lot?

What do they avoid saying?

How do they defend their views and sell their ideas?

How do they act under pressure?

After studying hundreds of people in the public eye alongside thousands more in my personal and professional life, I have seen the common denominators between those who are truly charismatic and those who aren't. I've carefully selected examples where these individuals have used their c-skills in high-stakes situations to help you learn.

What does Charisma Look Like at Uni?

In the same way elections separate good and bad charisma in politicians, graduate interviews act as a similar litmus test for undergraduates. Seeing how others at my university faired in the graduate job race helped me pin point those with good c-skills.

In my year group at university, there was a cohort of ultra-keen individuals who I thought would have been snapped up by employers with both hands. You know the type: The ones who always raise their hands at career events and somehow have 2 years work experience at big companies when they're the same age as everyone else! Surprisingly, many of them didn't fare much better than me.

My attention moved over to a handful of people who were absolutely killing it. They were landing offers left, right and centre at top companies—hedge funds, investment banks, tech giants and fast-growing start-ups. I had no idea what they were doing. At face value, they were not so different from me. Most were on track for second class honours and had good A-levels. Some had work experience some did not. It's only as I got to know them did I finally understand why they were doing so well.

These people carried themselves in a different way to everyone else. From one conversation, you respect and trust them at the same time. They were very secure within themselves, and even though they weren't the loudest in the room, everyone listened to them.

Their c-skills had a positive effect on other areas of their life too. They were confident and articulate speakers who had no issue winning over girls or guys they were attracted too. They got top positions in university societies. It even helped them achieve good grades. One particular person had a knack for getting close with key lecturers and students from the year above, putting him at a great advantage over everyone else. He used those relationships to gain a better understanding of what they were looking for in exams. He later went on to achieve the highest mark in his year, studied a masters degree at Cambridge and secured a position at a top investment bank in Hong Kong.

The common denominator between all of them was the belief that they were young adults not students. They accepted that to get to where they wanted, they needed to up their game and focus on every aspect of their repertoire. They were far from perfect, but they were not in denial about their strengths and weaknesses. I think many people at university are in this limbo phase between being a kid and an adult.

A kid gets told what to do and when to do it. A young adult looks at everything they may need to do, picks the most important tasks and then executes them. A kid waits for something to go wrong before rectifying it. A young adult asks questions, anticipates problems and solves them before they cause any damage. A kid has to ask others where the lecture is, a young adult knows this the day before.

I adopted this attitude and it benefited me in ways I never thought it would. It forced me to face-up to my weaknesses and do something about them. I turned from a timid kid who could barely maintain eye contact to someone who could impress managing directors at top companies with my confidence and leadership skills.

This is what I want for you. I want you to figure out where the gaps are in your c-skills, learn how to manage any social anxiety and prepare yourself for life after education. Seeing yourself as a young adult rather than a kid doesn't mean you'll become more boring or uninteresting. It's not about taking yourself more seriously. Rather, it's about accepting that you have flaws just like everyone else and are ready to improve yourself through whatever means necessary. When it comes to improving your c-skills, your first step is the most difficult and emotionally draining as you need to objectively measure your personality and ability to influence others.

Chapter 9
Measure your C-Skills

My company, Academic Underdogs, gathered the results of 200 third-year undergraduates from various universities and found that 68% of them felt their study skills or i-skills were better than their c-skills. We also conducted an independent poll of 400 third-year university students in the UK asking them if they felt stronger in their i-skills than c-skills. Over 72% said they felt stronger in their i-skills.

There is a reason for this.

Unlike the American education system, where students gain credit from sports and extra-curricular activity, the UK education system is almost exclusively exam focused. It rewards students with good i-skills and takes very little notice of those with strong c-skills. This breeds introversion.

Think about your time in college or 6th form. Apart from the odd exception, most of the time you were probably doing solitary activities such as homework, revision and coursework. With all this 'alone time', is there any surprise your c-skills were neglected?

In addition, we have no way to assess our c-skills properly. If you achieve Ds and Es in your A-levels, you know that your i-skills need to improve. But it's a different story with c-skills. There are no formal c-skill exams and no parent-teacher meeting where the teacher says, "Your son needs to improve his conversation skills and self-confidence otherwise he won't get into university".

This is why so many have an 'oh crap' moment when applying for jobs. Interviews and assessment centres are the only real way to examine your c-skills. Unfortunately, more often than not, these experiences come very late in life.

This is why, regardless of what year you are in or how extroverted you think you are, I recommend objectively testing your c-skills by applying for internships or work experience positions.

The C-Skills Test: The Interview

Just like an exam measures your i-skills, an interview at a top firm can measure your c-skills. I recommend attending an interview nice and early during university, even if you have no immediate plans to start working after your final year. An interview at a top organisation like Goldman Sachs, Diageo, Reckitt Benckiser, or any other FTSE 100 company, is ideal. Usually, the better the company, the harder the interviews and assessments are. Interviews with university admissions tutors or part-time jobs are nothing compared to the assessments at big branded companies. These firms invest millions of pounds in their human resource departments to separate the weak from the strong.

Graduate interviewers have very little to assess you on. Most graduates have had little to no professional experience and haven't had enough time outside of education to really shine at something. They do consider your grades and your university, but their final decision is largely based on your personality. This is why interviews are much better litmus tests than personality questionnaires or other psychoanalysis tools.

After a few assessment days or interviews you will learn a lot about yourself. I fell flat on my face in my first interview and I took it very personally. The feedback I received was sugar coated and mentioned something about my leadership skills, but it all came down to the fact they didn't like my personality. It was frustrating because I couldn't control my nerves so I didn't get to show my personality.

With charisma, half the battle is getting out of your own head!

These early interviews scared the living daylights out of me. After my ego recovered, I knew my entire repertoire of skills needed to improve quickly otherwise I would end up on benefits my whole life. It was a dramatic conclusion in hindsight, but I believed it at the time.

It was painful to learn all this about myself but also very necessary. My priorities changed and I began taking proactive steps towards building my confidence. This included research around anxiety management as well as proactive exercises I'd set myself in casual social settings. All of this helped me improve over the course of a few months.

With my current university mentees, who are struggling with confidence and social issues, my first piece of advice is always the same: get yourself into an interview room ASAP. Not only will you give yourself a chance to land some good experience and a brand on your CV, but it will also be the first real test of your c-skills.

Chapter 10
What's to Come

Imagine how different your life would be if people noticed you every time you walked into a room; if they hung on every word you said and sought your approval for every move they made. Those with excellent c-skills experience this all the time. They tend to get what they want, are paid more, receive more attention on social media, and have more romantic options.

Simply put, better c-skills unlock better opportunities.

It may seem like these c-skill masters naturally exude charisma and confidence, as if it's an innate, subconscious reaction, but while that's true for some people, it's not the case for everyone.

Although they would never admit it the most skilled individuals, including politicians and celebrities, consciously behave in a way that makes them more likeable and persuasive. Many prolific figures have 'social coaches' whose job it is to improve their public image by carefully crafting their personalty. Spin doctors, life coaches, motivation experts—call them what you will, their purpose is the same. They're there to teach their clients how to be more likeable and how to command more respect.

That's also where I come in—I'm going to be your coach! By describing practical and actionable methods you can use in your everyday life, you'll improve the subconscious and conscious areas of your persona. I'm not asking you to completely change your personality, but rather to build your own style around the methods that I describe. Doing so will improve the way your tutors, employers, colleagues and friends treat you, which in turn will provide you with better prospects in your education, career and relationships.

With charisma, there is no finite formula because being charismatic requires a certain sense of individuality. Charismatic people stand out for the right reasons and project their personality in the correct way. However, you can learn and practice several core ideas that you can build your personality around.

50% of the journey is managing your emotions and social anxiety. As you'll learn later, social anxiety is unique in that it's the only anxiety that never goes away completely. It has to be kept at bay continuously through proactive means. Social anxiety is like a memory foam mattress—you can push it down but it gradually comes back to where it was.

Three Pillars of Charisma

Chapter 11
Presence

Emma: *"That homework was hard, wasn't it?"*

Fatima: *"Still haven't finished it and don't think I will. I need an excuse. Maybe the old 'my dog ate it' will work. It's a cliché for a reason, right? Then again, poor Buster is in a dog hotel while my parents are on holiday".*

(half an hour later)

Fatima: *"How is your boyfriend?"*

Emma: *"He has really been getting on my nerves lately—do you think there are any more vacancies in that dog hotel?"*

Emma & Fatima: *"LOL"*

Emma was truly present in the conversation and remembered the passing comment Fatima made about her dog half an hour earlier. Interactions like this are what create trust and friendship between people. We've all experienced moments like this before. How good does it feel to know that the person you're speaking to is truly present and listening?

Presence

Presence is essential to becoming admired and respected.

Unfortunately, being continuously present for long periods of time is actually quite difficult. It's annoyingly easy to become distracted and this isn't our fault. We have evolved to be twitchy and have a fleeting attention span. Our ancestors used this to spot the movement of a sabre tooth tiger or grazing deer, and they were better survivors as a result. Unfortunately, unless you're an athlete, this characteristic is more of a hindrance than a blessing today.

Have you ever stopped listening halfway through a conversation and started nodding your head in agreement even though you've completely lost track of what the other person is saying? While distracted, did you start worrying if the other person knows you're not listening? Did worrying make the situation worse and stop you from listening even more? When the other person stopped talking, did you panic over what you should say next?!

If you've been through this sequence before, chances are the person you were speaking to had an idea that you weren't present. We all instinctively know when someone else isn't listening to us and this is why we become paranoid about being caught day dreaming. We're not mind readers, however, so how does this work?

It mostly comes down to facial expressions. The human brain is capable of reading facial expressions in as little as seventeen milliseconds.

When our minds start wondering mid-conversation, the slightly delayed reactions in our face and changes to our pupil size can give it all away. So, what can we do to stop dozing off and start being better listeners? One way is to continuously remind ourselves that every person is an opportunity.

One Relationship Can Change your Life

Every person you cross paths with is a potential friend, partner, colleague or customer. They can all have some impact on your life that you have yet to discover. By not being present during any given conversation, you're passing up the opportunity of finding out what your relationship could turn into.

Some of the most amazing accomplishments have been achieved on the back of a single relationship. Take the invention of smartphones as an example. Imagine if back when Steve Jobs met Steve Wozniak, Jobs 'couldn't be bothered' or failed to look past Woz's nerdiness and physical appearance. He could have easily written him off and we'd all still be using Nokias! Instead, he focused on Woz's ability to build computers and that excited him.

Don't ever underestimate how a single relationship can change your life!

Whether it's a trade show with several thousand people or a party full of strangers, I always take a moment to look at the crowd and remind myself of the opportunities. It stops me from becoming cynical and, more importantly, socially lazy.

Once you've got your head out of your ass, it becomes much easier to engage in conversation and be present. Then all you need to do is keep your emotions in check. People who are ego driven feel jealous or insecure when meeting others who are more successful, skilled or better looking than them. These are low level emotions that hinder your c-skills. Being inspired by people is the best way to push these emotions aside. You can't admire someone and be jealous of them at the same time! Remain present by giving people the benefit of the doubt—focus on their strengths rather than their weaknesses and always be curious.

There are other more practical steps we can take to improve our focus and attentiveness, including mindfulness meditation.

Mindfulness Mediation

Meditation and mindfulness are common buzzwords at the moment. For me, these have been a part of my life since I was four years old. I consider myself a bit of an expert! Both of these terms refer to a technique that helps you focus on the present moment. If you've ever kept track of your thoughts over a single day, you will have noticed that most of the time you were either looking over your shoulder at the past or ahead into the future. The past is full of memories, some negative and some positive. The future is full of simulations, often in the form of fears or concerns. Meditation helps you drop all of these thoughts, if only for a moment, and to enjoy the here and now.

How does this help our charisma and ability to stay present?

Regular meditation improves our ability to focus and to avoid being at the mercy of careless thoughts and concerns. Try something for me right now. Sit on a chair or lie back on your bed, close your eyes and try not to think about anything. Attempt this for about thirty seconds.

Difficult, right? Did you notice how thoughts just enter your head uninvited? Sometimes it feels like we're the author of our own thoughts when we actually have limited control. This is why it's difficult to focus on a task for long periods of time and why it's easy to doze off during conversations. We can never stop this from happening completely, however, we can improve our ability to focus through regular meditation. But, does it really work? Having meditated for so many years, I can personally vouch that it *does* work. I have complimented my ability to focus on a task intently. If you aren't convinced, the scientific community also found strong evidence that supports the link between meditation and increased focus.

Five independent research papers compared candidates who practiced mindfulness techniques with those that didn't. Tests designed to measure sustained attention showed that individuals who practiced meditation performed better. Candidates were better at adapting to surprise changes in the tasks given to them, they processed distractions quicker, and they showed a greater ability to focus on a task for a sustained period of time. If we think of our brains as computers, regular meditation seems to give us more RAM and help us pay attention to others.

Mindfulness mediation is a proactive way of approaching the problem. However, what can we do in the moment when we catch ourselves dozing off?

Snapping Back

When you do inevitably become distracted mid-conversation, focus on your breathing or the sensations in your hands for a split second and get back in again. Another technique I personally use is the 'Eyelash Snap' where you focus on your conversation partner's eye until it blinks and then snap yourself back into focus.

Presence

That warm fuzzy feeling you create for others when they realise that you've been listening, coupled with the understanding you achieve by paying attention are fundamental to charisma. Without presence, everything else in this book becomes useless.

In the Charisma Project at the end of the book, I'll give you a step by step guide on how to meditate. I'll also give you some best practices that I learnt from a number of experts including monks in Japan and free-diving coaches in Indonesia! Now, let's look at the second pillar of Charisma.

Chapter 12
Authority

After rushing out of Chancery Lane Station at 7:30 AM I walked into the 23rd day of my summer internship at one of the top investment banks in the city, oblivious to what was about to happen. My manager was several months pregnant, overworked, frustrated and hormonal. Unfortunately for me, she was in a particularly bad mood this day and I had made a mistake the day before which had come to her attention at 7:39; one minute before I walked into the office.

She let me say hello to the rest of the team before starting:

'Why on earth did you CC him when I told you NOT TO?!'

'Do YOU want this job or NOT?'

'THIS JUST ISN'T GOOD ENOUGH'

She was becoming more enraged with every sentence and I could see she was going to let rip in front of the entire floor just as she'd done a few weeks before to David, my colleague and fellow summer intern.

When this happened to David, he just stood there, head down and eyes wide as she dismantled him for the tiniest mistake. His whole body closed in on itself and he was left speechless. David was never the same after that day and I didn't want that to happen to me too. So, in that moment, I decided to react in the exact opposite way I usually would.

Instead of shying away, I planted my feet and moved my body to face her. I looked her dead in the face and kept my eyes small to avoid looking like a deer in headlights. Surprisingly, my feeling of shock and discomfort faded. Usually at this point my body would go into fight or flight mode, even though I wasn't in any physical danger. In response to adrenaline, my eyes would dilate to maximise light flow into my retina and increase my awareness. My brain would make me swallow in case there was anything in my windpipe that would stop me from escaping a harmful situation. Everyone around me would see my Adam's apple move and know that I was panicking. None of that happened this time and I stood still, listening as she went full force.

After she was done, I kept my gaze and paused for at least four seconds before responding:

Me: *"I understand why you're angry. Do you mind if we have a 5-minute catch up and I'll be happy to explain?"*

Manager: *"Do you really think I want to waste any more time on you?"*

Me: *"Fair enough. Sorry for the mistake—I'll be more careful next time"*

There was no stutter or mumble in my voice and I spoke clearly while maintaining eye contact. Surprisingly, my manager was the one looking away and she sounded a little defeated. I immediately sat down at my desk, picked up my phone and started working on the first task on my to-do list. Everyone else in my team looked at me, shocked at how I'd just weathered the storm and continued with my work like nothing happened. Inside I was still feeling a little embarrassed and humiliated, but on the outside, apparently, I looked rock solid.

"You are one cool cucumber".

"I respect you for the way you handled that – good on you".

"If that was me, I would be in the bathroom in tears right now".

These were some of the comments my colleagues said to me later in the day. People respected me for how I didn't crack under pressure. All I did was choose how I wanted to react rather than let my body run its usual course. Everything was different after this incident. The smiles were wider when I walked into the office, everyone, my manager included, was more willing to sacrifice their time to help me and I was first to be invited out.

Had I curled up into a little ball, it would have revealed weakness. Lashing out or shouting back at my manager would have masked my embarrassment and demonstrated some authority, but I would have also lost my job. On this occasion, I got the balance just right and learned that I could still be authoritative even if I didn't have authority.

This wasn't the last time I came under this kind of pressure. With each situation, in both my personal and professional life, I developed a thicker skin and a belief that I could handle any setback.

How to Develop Authority

Many people fake authority and this can work in the short term. However, true and authentic authority is built by continuously leaping into uncomfortable situations and then climbing out. By pushing your limits again and again, your pain thresholds will increase and you will develop this unwavering belief that no matter what happens you will be OK. If you get sacked, you can find another job. If your girl or boyfriend dumps you, you can recover from the emotional hurt and find someone else. Even if you don't find anyone, you'll be happy being single.

Speak to anyone in the military who has served on the front line and you'll notice an aura of authority in the way they speak and act. If you put them in a situation that you or I might find terrifying, like a panel interview or meeting your girlfriend's parents, they would manage it quite easily. Some grilling from a poker-faced vice president is nothing compared to putting your life on the line in a war zone.

Once you truly believe that nothing can hurt you, authority will ooze out of every word you say and from your body language. Unfortunately, you can't choose what to believe. You either believe in something or you don't. Either the evidence satisfies you or it doesn't. We all have an internal gauge of what is true and false. This is why there are no shortcuts when it comes to developing authority and you'll need to proactively improve over time.

Doing so will put you ahead of the curve in the medium-to-long term. Some of the 'anti-comfort zone' tasks I set for you in the Charisma Project will produce noticeable changes after a few months. Meanwhile, there are other techniques and habits you can adopt to project more authority in the short term. These include posture, voice tonality, clothing, external distractions and generally knowing what authoritative behaviour looks like.

Hopefully by the end of this book, you will be inspired to take action towards developing this area of your charisma. Eventually, you won't need to fake anything to anyone. Provided you don't become arrogant, people who are less secure and confident will gravitate towards you.

Why Authority is Attractive?

When meeting someone for the first time, our conscious and subconscious minds continuously try to figure out how they can benefit us. Again, this is hardwired into us from years of evolution. Our ancestors viewed physical strength, resources and influence over others as indicators of authority or power. Even though none of these characteristics are really needed for survival now, we're still attracted to individuals that have them.

There is no surprise that the number one question you'll hear now is, 'What university do you go to?' or 'What course do you do?'. After university it will turn into, 'What do you do?' You can argue that it's just small talk, but the main purpose of that question is to size one another up. We could rephrase those questions more bluntly to 'How intelligent are you?' or 'How much money and resources do you have?' or 'Are you in a position of power?'. Sounds shallow? Blame it on our ancestors!

While the logical parts of our minds are probing for social information, the emotional parts are busy gathering clues from body language. If someone is meeting you for the first time, they won't know where you sit in the social pecking order so what do they do? They make assumptions based on what they hear and see. Extended eye contact will lead them to assume that you have good intentions. A confident posture will lead them to assume you have something to be confident about. Whatever you project, they will accept and believe.

You need to be careful though as showing only authority will push people away. Many people will respect you but you may come across unapproachable or unlikable. Authority has to be balanced with affection.

Chapter 13
Affection

Affection is simply projecting to the world that it's OK to come and say hello. Do people say that 'you're always in a good mood' or that 'you smile a lot'? If so, that's a good sign that you project affection to those around you. Some people, guys and girls, naturally have RBF (Resting Bitch Face) where their default facial expression is one of seriousness or moodiness. If you have RBF, you'll find that people are standoffish and cautious around you. Smiling more and physically touching others in an appropriate fashion will solve this problem!

Affection is also projected through your attentiveness to other people's feelings. Small gestures like making eye contact with a shy new member of a group may seem like they go unnoticed, but they don't. Helping others escape embarrassment is another way to be attentive.

At a dinner with my girlfriend's family, her brother-in-law accidentally revealed that everyone had planned a surprise birthday party for her dad. After realising what he'd done after the dinner, his face turned bright red with embarrassment in front of the group. To take the heat off him I said:

"Good thing I forgot about the surprise birthday otherwise I would have said the exact same thing as you!"

Everyone laughed at my comment and it took the attention off him immediately. Later in the evening when we were saying our goodbyes, he said:

"You're a top guy—I've got a good feeling about you".

He wasn't a very affectionate person so this initially took me by surprise. However, immediately after making this comment, he gave me a slightly confused look as if to say he didn't know why that even came out of his mouth. I knew exactly where it came from and why he said it!

Bailing people out of small holes they've accidentally dug themselves into, and being attentive, will show people that you have empathy and are emotionally intelligent. Subconsciously they'll think 'if this guy is attentive enough to help me out on such a tiny problem, he must be willing to help me out in other ways too'. From an evolutionary perspective, this is the basis behind why we find affectionate people attractive.

Why Affection is Attractive?

Even though there are many aspects of our personalities which we can adapt over time through our experiences, there are some which are hardwired into us through millions of years of evolution. Our genetic need to reproduce and survive subtly governs our choices every single day, particularly when picking friends.

We tend to surround ourselves with people who sacrifice for us or have the potential to do so in the future. This is because our great, great, great, great x100 grandparents knew that they had a better chance of surviving if they had friends who provided resources or safety for them. Knowing if the person on their left and right were able and *willing* to fight off a sabre tooth tiger was a life and death decision. As a result, we are sensitive to affectionate body language and other social behaviour that says 'I can and will sacrifice for you'.

Chapter 14
Judgement Chart

We continuously and often unknowingly emit signals and body language to those around us, and people judge us based on these signals. This can be a difficult to accept, but the truth is, we all emit, we all judge—it's a reflex we can't control.

Living in fear of judgement is like having a phobia to sunlight. The only way to avoid your fear is to become a hermit, to avoid any situations which may bring harm, no matter how innocuous they seem to others.

Instead of shying away we should embrace it and understand how people develop their perceptions. Only then can you join the minority of people who have truly mastered the art of charisma and are able to breeze through life seemingly unaffected.

The Judgement Chart

Inside all of our minds, there is a tiny caveman standing in front of hundreds of flip charts with a graph on it that looks like this:

Judgement Chart

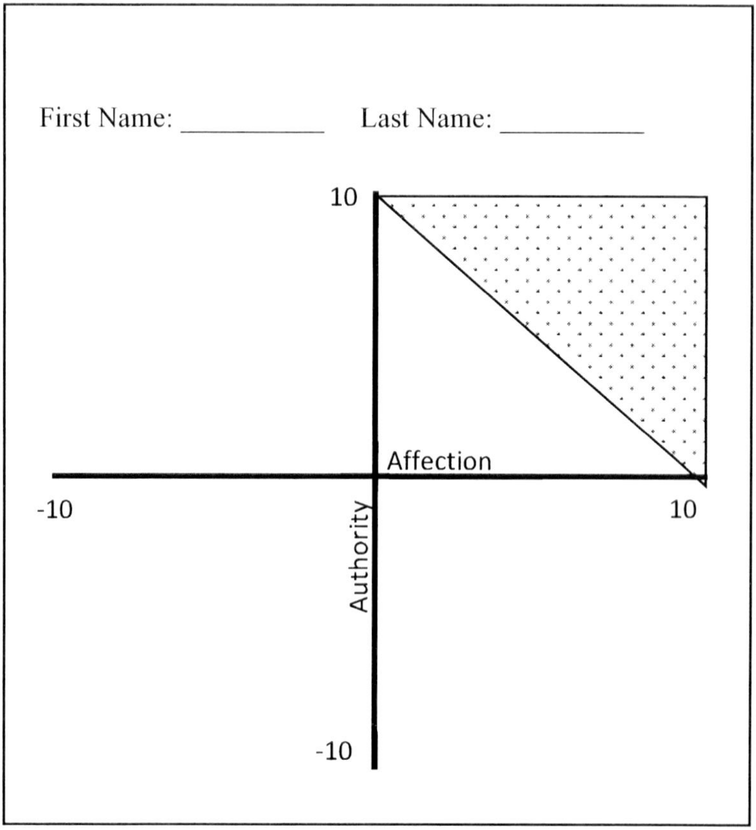

There is one of these for each person you know, including those you haven't met personally. There are charts for characters you've seen on Netflix boxsets; people you encounter on your commuter; and even your mother.

That little caveman is responsible for plotting the data that your senses pass to him. Every time you meet, see, hear about, listen to, touch or even think about someone this caveman gets to work. He processes all the data, plots it and provides you with an average score that defines your judgement. This chart is dynamic and your judgement can change depending on the data you receive.

To be a charismatic person who is both admired and respected, you need to project a high level of affection and authority in the **majority** of your social interactions. In other words, you need to stay in the top right-hand corner of the judgement chart as much as possible. This is called the **Charisma Zone**.

By projecting both of these characteristics, that cavemen will be telling their hosts…

'this person has influence and they seem willing to help'

Getting this balance consistently wrong will reduce your charisma.

Too much authority and you can come across intimidating and unapproachable; too much affection and you may seem desperate for approval.

Now, I'm fully aware that I've just massively oversimplified the very complex fields of human psychology and neuroscience. Each judgement chart, in reality, has multiple dimensions which psychologists have been studying and speculating over for a very long time. I'm sure there will be one or two psychologists firing shots at me in the Amazon reviews. However, for the purpose of this book, deep granular theory won't be useful or add any practical value to you.

First Judgement

Several decades ago, the only way someone could develop a first impression of you without actually meeting you face-to-face was from word-of-mouth. Now all they need to do is google your name.

Stacy is about to start her course at the same university as Fred. After browsing through an online group for freshers, she came across Fred's Instagram account. Within a few seconds her cavewoman has already plotted several data points on his judgement chart:

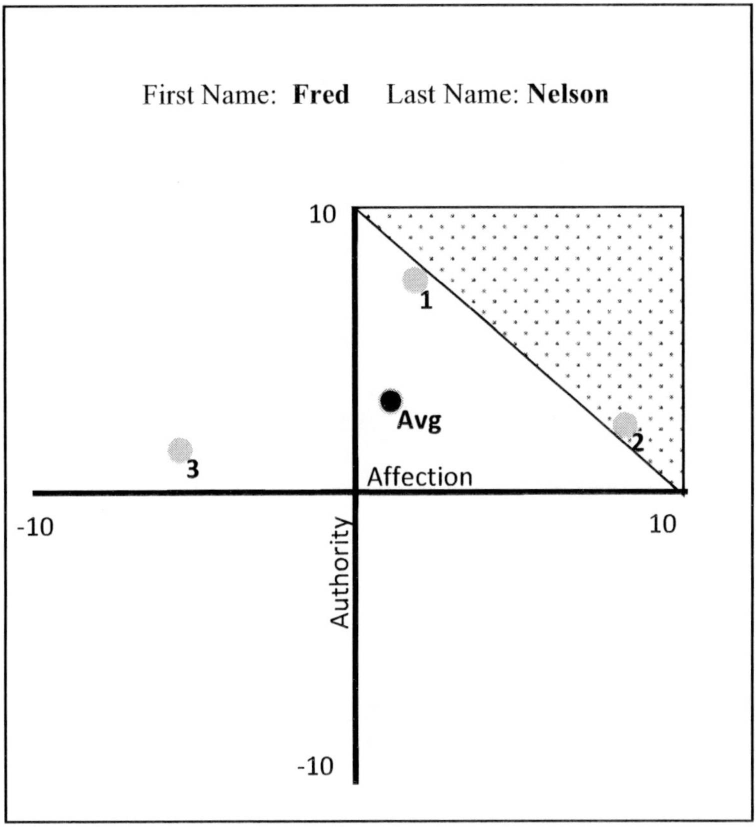

1. Video of Fred speaking in front of a crowd of people
2. Picture of Fred hugging his parents
3. Offensive comment Fred made on a picture

Stacy's judgement of Fred will be an average based on her interpretation of what she sees on his Instagram page. This will, of course, be a 'weighted average' as we all have different biases and lenses through which we assess the world. Some people are very cynical, others tend to hold very strong political views. These all play a part in judgement. We can't control other people's biases; however, we can detect them and work around them if need be.

Second Judgement

On the first day of university, Fred walks into the induction room sits down right next to Stacy. She spots him as soon as he walks into the room and her cavewoman gets to work again. If we could see an audit trail of her thoughts, it would look something like this:

00:00:01 Nice t-shirt
00:00:02 Smiling
00:00:03 Small forehead
00:00:04 Little shorter than I expected
00:00:05 Never seen eyebrows that shape before
00:00:06 Keeps looking down

.

.

.

As you can see, Stacy produces both negative and positive judgements about Fred. They are very shallow too! He can't exactly change the size of his forehead or height, can he?!
This is human nature at its best and worst. Judging others is a very important trait that helps us anticipate the moves of others and we need it to succeed in our relationships. However, an

unfortunate by-product of being judgmental creatures is that we will always be judged according to our looks and other characteristics that we have little control over. We need to embrace judgement, not resent it. Fortunately, there are plenty of characteristics that we *can* control that hold much more weight than the thickness of our eyebrows.

Fred read this book, practiced my techniques and has developed excellent c-skills. After speaking with Stacey for 10 minutes, her judgement chart of him now looks like this:

Today

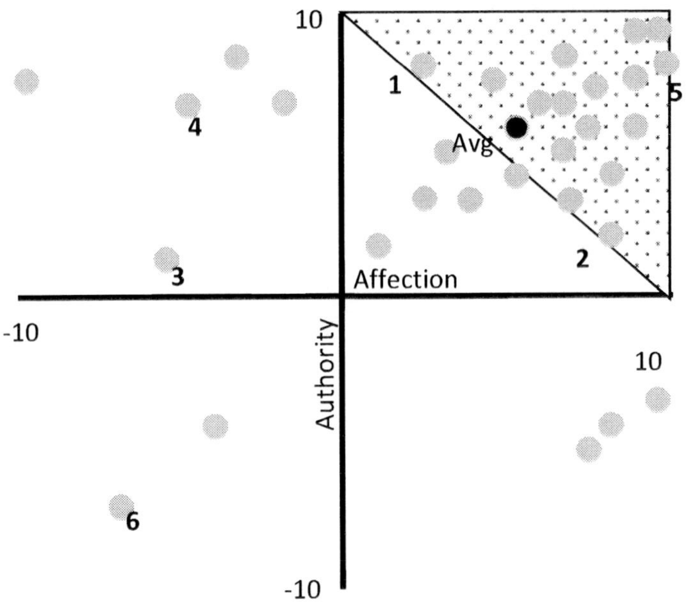

1. Leant back on his chair with your arm resting on the chair next to him
2. Defended a student who was slightly humiliated by another student in front of the whole year group
3. Distasteful, unfunny and borderline sexist joke

No social interaction is going to be perfect. Body language is misinterpreted and miscommunicated just as much as verbal language. Messing up is normal! You will fumble, mumble, doze off, tell bad jokes and offend people for the rest of your life. It doesn't matter—so will everyone else! Whenever you embarrass yourself in public, don't give up and write yourself off. Be brave, relentless and keep projecting your personality and charisma Your average score matters more than the last social hiccup.

Tomorrow Stacy will forget most of her judgements and all but one data point will remain on her judgement chart—the average.

Tomorrow

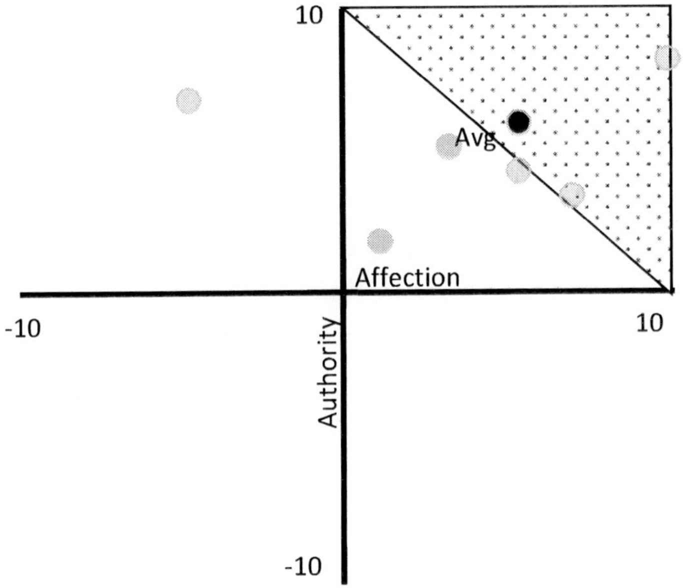

This average score will be her final judgement of Fred until they cross paths again. This entire time, Fred has also built an average score for Stacy and this too happens to be in the charisma zone. This is what 'clicking' with someone looks like. Truly charismatic people can detect when they are not in the zone, make necessary adjustments to their body and verbal language and eventually 'click' with almost anyone.

Staying in the Zone

Let's say you are the floor manager at a clothing store and you've hired a brand-new sales assistant called Bella. From Bella's perspective, you're dominant and already have authority by default without even opening your mouth. If you only want her respect, then you're right where you want to be. If you want her to like and respect you, which you should do if you want to influence them, you will need to display a little more affectionate behaviour to keep yourself in the charisma zone.

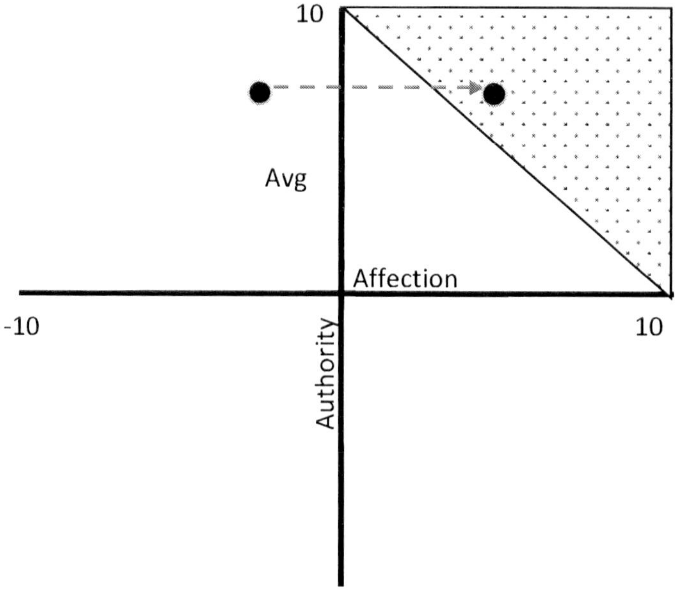

Over time you might overdo it with affection, lose authority and fall out of the charisma zone. Bella might then take advantage and start turning up late, thinking they can get away with it. Or, maybe she we will stop giving you her full attention when you're speaking to her. Usually, obvious and less obvious signals will show you where you stand with Bella and reading these signals is critical. To get yourself back in the charisma zone, you may need to be firmer with your tone or project dominant body language during a team meeting.

Reading how people perceive you and making subtle adjustments is second nature to those who are truly admired and respected.

Outlier Situations – When you are Under Attack

Sometimes the charisma zone isn't the right place to be. There are one-off situations where you shouldn't show any affection whatsoever. For example, if you are being taken advantage of or insulted by someone in a malicious way, you should only be showing authority.

Remember the bully in your high school? On the first day of school, they tap you on the back of the head as they walk past your chair and you let it go. Next week, that tap turns into a jab. Again, you laugh it off and show no authority. A month later, he walks into the classroom and you expect some kind of contact. Maybe another tap? He walks past your chair. Phew, you're in the clear! You turn around to check, only to see a sweaty palm traveling towards you—SLAP! As your ears stop ringing, you hear laughter coming from all directions and see the entire class revelling in your misery!

Showing authority is sometimes the best option and being neutral or showing any affection whatsoever doesn't work in your favour. Luckily, this altercation was all a dream, and tomorrow it all plays out in real life. This time you stand up from your chair the very first time he taps you. Then you square up to the bully with your shoulders back, you look him dead in the eye and tell him to fuck off.

Chances are, no one will be physically abusing you at university or after graduation. However, you will be on the receiving end of emotional or verbal abuse at some point in the future. Make sure you don't tolerate this and react accordingly to prevent it from going too far.

Outlier Situations – When you Need to be Vulnerable

"I can't stop thinking about her, no matter how much I try"

My close friend, Aman, was long overdue a heart to heart conversation after his girlfriend ended their relationship a few weeks back. Myself and another close friend, Fawaz, listened closely in the living room of Aman's flat as he brought up the topic.

Aman, like most guys, wasn't comfortable showing his emotions to anyone, let alone his guy-friends. My objective was to let Aman know that we would be discreet and he could speak freely without judgement. Ultimately, I wanted to help him heal and get over his ex.

So, I sat down next to him and closed-up my body language by leaning forward. This reduced my authority. By reassuring him that it's OK to be honest with us and exposing the palms of my hands as I spoke, I projected more affection. None of these changes in my body language were conscious at the time. When you learn and think about your c-skills regularly, you start behaving in the correct way instinctively.

Ultimately, it worked. He opened up:

"I feel really betrayed by the way she ended things with us. We were together for ages. I can't believe she was so cold towards me"

At this point Fawaz became uncomfortable and started walking around the room, busying himself with whatever distraction he could find. He finished his beer abnormally fast and went to the kitchen to get a new one. Then, he moved positions from the sofa arm rest to the radiator. Eventually, he stood over Aman with his hands on his waist in a very authoritative fashion! Make no mistake, Fawaz is a top guy, but he is a typical emotionally distant male who doesn't know how to manage his own emotions let alone anyone else's. Aman felt judged, so he avoided eye contact with Fawaz and eventually changed the subject.

"Screw her. I can't be arsed to talk about it...lets go out"

Low and behold, Aman called me the next day sounding even more distraught. Fawaz should have been more aware of his body language and what he was projecting, then he could have made the necessary adjustments, the conversation could have continued and I could have helped Aman to calm down.

By observing others with good c-skills and reading books like this you can learn how to react in outlier situations. Fawaz and I were in almost an identical scenario with another friend recently. This time he projected more affection than authority and it did the trick!

Judgement Chart

Authority and affection are parameters you can use to score your 'performance' during high-stakes social situations. I do this almost every day, especially after interactions with people in my professional life. If I got into an altercation with a supplier or key stakeholder in my business:

"Was I right or wrong? If I knew I was right, why did I let them talk over me? Next time, show more authority."

If I couldn't close a sale:

"Were they happy with the price? Yes. Were they in the right part of their buying cycle? Yes. So why didn't I close? I qualified myself and the business clearly and showed the right amount of authority. Maybe that last comment came across as too arrogant and I should have leaned forward and smiled as I said it?"

This is the type of narrative that constantly runs through my head and the style of conversation I have with those close to me. My friends, family, colleagues and mentees speak to me regularly about high-stakes social situations that they've been a part of. We all coach each other using these parameters to give the conversation structure. This is what you should do too.

By approaching your relationships like an anthropologist and using the judgement chart as a scoring system, you will develop emotional intelligence faster than your peers. Building a strong network of people who you can bounce ideas off will accelerate your c-skills even more. Combine this feedback process with our Charisma Project and you will know when to project authority, affection or both.

As you've probably gathered by now, being admired and respected is about more than smiling lots or making eye contact. It comes down to understanding what charismatic and un-charismatic behaviour looks like; reading people or situations; keeping a memory bank of tools that increase your social value then deploying those tools when necessary.

Judgement Chart

There's a lot going on! Are we really capable of managing all these tasks at the same time and, if so, how do we do it?

Chapter 15
Social Instinct

In January 2014, there was a study done by MIT to see how well our subconscious minds detect subtle changes in body language. Men were shown images of women and asked to choose the most attractive. What the candidates didn't know was that the pupils in many of the women's eyes were Photoshopped to look wider. An astounding 70% of the men selected the Photoshopped images over the unedited ones. This happened because our pupils dilate when we are sexually aroused. Evolution has made our subconscious detect millimetre differences in pupil size to improve our chances of getting laid and reproducing.

Given our evolutionary past, the ability to detect and interpret subtle changes in body language comes as no surprise. Before humans invented language, this was the only way our ancestors could communicate. Thousands of years on, we still haven't parted from our evolutionary roots and are very perceptive to subtle changes in body language. This is why we need to do our very best to ensure the many hundreds of signals we display are associated with authority and affection. How many of these signals can we <u>consciously</u> control at the same time?

Why we Can't Multi-Task

One of the most viewed TED talks of all time happened in June 2013 when Apollo Robbins, the best pickpocket in the world, came on stage to expose one of our largest limitations as human beings: our inability to multi-task. He began by asking for a volunteer, Joe, to help him with his demonstration. Over the course of a few minutes he deceived the volunteer and the rest of the audience multiple times.

By getting everyone to focus on Joe's hand, he was able to move a poker chip to different points of his body without anyone noticing. He was also able to steal his watch, money and a shrimp he took from the buffet to eat later! Apollo, like many other pickpockets, made a career out of our uni-tasking processor brains.

Social Instinct

There are a bunch of social signals like pupil size that we can't consciously control. Of the signals that *can* be consciously controlled, we can only focus on one task at a time. No wonder people feel that body language training is pointless!

Given that we have all these limitations, what steps can we take towards making sure our body language lands us in the top right of the judgement chart without having to focus on a hundred tasks at once? By making sure we control whatever we can in our external environment and managing our internal emotions better.

How to be Admired & Respected

Stabilising the Pendulum

Chapter 16
External Distractions

Each and every one of us has a present, authoritative and affectionate person inside. However, sometimes that person doesn't emerge because of internal and external discomfort. Internal factors are those that originate in the mind and these include feelings of anxiety, insecurity, uncertainty and fear. Conversely, external factors originate outside the mind and include discomfort brought about from physical sensations or environment.

External Distractions

Oliver was a computer science undergraduate at the University of Leeds. He was hard working, had achieved great A-levels and was on track for a First. Having sent off multiple internship applications to several companies, his first breakthrough came when a managing director of a medium-sized company agreed to meet him for a casual interview.

This was Olly's first opportunity to get some valuable, paid work experience while opening the door to a full-time graduate position. He prepared for weeks; perfecting his answers, learning everything he could about the company. He even contacted other recent graduates who worked at the firm on

LinkedIn to gain a deeper understanding of their services and products.

On the interview day, the interviewer met Olly in a coffee shop in Central London around lunch time. It was very busy at the time so they grabbed the only table available, which happened to be right next to the coffee machines.

One of the first questions the interviewer asked him was:

'What do you know about our company and products we offer?'

This was Olly's moment to shine and make a brilliant first impression. He started explaining, but parts of his explanation kept being drowned out by customers, hissing machines and clanging metal. By repeating sentences, leaning forward and speaking louder, he made sure his answer was heard. However, this meant breaking eye contact and corrupting his body language. The frustration and uncertainty whether he was being heard or not caused tension to appear on his face; wrinkles and shadows on his forehead.

What was the interviewer thinking? Surely she understood and sympathised with Olly's discomfort, right? Wrong! The interviewer had no idea what was going on in his head so she made assumptions like: *Why does he seem so uptight? Maybe I shouldn't have asked this question so early?* His uptight appearance had nothing to do with the question but it distracted the interviewer and ruined her first impression.

Noisy environments are not the only external factors that can cause discomfort. Constipation, period pains, muscle injuries, uncomfortable clothing, clammy crotch, hot or cold environment—even the sun can be your enemy at a time like this.

Halfway through a date on a rooftop terrace the sun broke through the clouds, and its beams hit me directly in the face. I ended up squinting for the entire time we were up there. For the second half of the date, I noticed a change in her demeanour. Even though we continued chatting normally, she asked out of the blue whether I was enjoying the date. I asked her why and she said:

"Just had a feeling that you weren't".

Squinting and eyebrow-clenching is not a good look! She thought my look of discomfort was her fault. Our reaction to external discomfort and internal discomfort is the same. Unless informed otherwise, people assume something's wrong and that it has something to do with them. This happens because we all have a tendency to think the world revolves around us.

Think back to a time when you were on your own in an area with a group of others you didn't know and they suddenly burst into laughter. Was your knee jerk reaction to assume they were laughing at you? In actual fact, they were probably laughing at a joke. What about a time when someone yawned during a conversation with you. Did you worry that you were boring

them? Chances are they were tired or happened to have too much CO_2 in their lungs at that moment.
We're all sensitive to external distractions. There was an experiment where individuals were handed a cup of coffee and asked to read a passage from a short story. Half of these individuals were handed ice-cold coffee and the other hot coffee. 80% of the ice-coffee group gave a negative opinion on the character while 80% of the hot-coffee group gave the opposite opinion. Whether we like it or not, our internal thoughts and feelings are affected by external stimuli.

Technology is also a big distraction. Many feel that tech is destroying face-to-face social skills and preventing us from building meaningful relationships. This isn't a new problem and we only need to look around us to see the evidence. A waiting room without a TV on the wall will be filled with more conversation than one with a 20-inch plasma. Two people in a car would chat more if there wasn't a radio or music system. Now a technological distraction has found itself in our pockets and we carry it around with us everywhere we go.

Blaming smart phones or social media is pointless. There will always be external distractions. We just need to identify them and build good habits that stop them affecting our charisma.

For example, continuously checking your phone when you're speaking to someone breaks eye contact and shows them that you are not present. Immediately placing your phone on the table after sitting down reveals your true priorities. Also, do you ever go on your phone when you're feeling awkward around people you don't know very well? You're not the only one. Phones play to the introvert in all of us, giving us an excuse to remove ourselves from social situations and the potential awkward feelings they elicit, but this stifles our social skills.

Next time you walk into a waiting room notice how others take out their phones and use them as a social life raft.

Many of my mentees mention how smartphones have made it difficult to initiate conversations. One of them said:

"If I see someone on their phone, I assume they are busy and I use that excuse not to say hello."

No one wants to be rejected! Most of the time people are on their phones passing time. They are either checking their social feed, binge reading or watching a video. Remember that next time you're waiting outside a lecture theatre with a bunch of strangers and your phone is burning a hole in your pocket, you *do* have a choice. One may lead to successfully finding a new meme. The other a new conversation and potentially a relationship or opportunity!

Reducing External Distractions:

Unlike internal distractions, external ones are much easier to control especially if you know where to look.

1. Scope out three suitable venues when preparing for a high-stakes meeting

Let's say you've been chasing down a senior member of staff at an organisation you're interested in, and she finally calls and asks where to meet you. You should never be 'umming' and 'ahhing' or telling her to 'meet at a station and find somewhere'. Always scope out restaurants, bars or coffee shops beforehand.

Ideally, these should be places you're familiar with. Knowing the busy periods, layout, menu, best tables and even some of the staff will give you an edge. Pick places where you can reserve tables as well.

Having moved around a lot over the past few years, scoping out suitable venues has been a top priority. After finding a couple places, I tend to visit them multiple times with friends and make sure the staff know who I am. Some people think this is a bit over-the-top. However, that's how much effort I put in to achieve a social edge. I know for a fact that others are equally if not more pedantic than I am, including some of the most successful people I know.

2. Wear clothing which is both fashionable and comfortable

Hipster is in—unfortunately! Tight shirts, jeans and skirts look great but are serious external distractions. Restrictive tops are particularly bad. As you'll learn in chapter 26, speaking from the chest and maintaining a baritone voice is an essential way of projecting authority. You may not notice just as you put a tight shirt on, but over time, it will stop your chest from expanding out. Your breath will become shallow and your voice higher pitched. Keep this in mind before buying new clothes or choosing something from your current wardrobe.

3. Personal hygiene and medical

Fabrics are also worth keeping an eye on. Certain materials like silk and synthetics make you sweat more. Some of my friends have seen women drying their underarms under dryers in public bathrooms and I personally know one guy who sticks sanitary pads down his sleeves! Get yourself some stronger antiperspirant on Amazon or avoid wearing dodgy fabrics when the stakes are high.

The same goes for any other personal hygiene or medical issues you may have. What foods upset your stomach? Do you tend to get migraines and headaches? What allergies do you have? You know your body better than anyone else. Do what you need to do!

Of course, sometimes no matter how much we try, unexpected discomforts can pop up. One of my friends has irritable bowel syndrome. It causes uncontrollable stomach pain no matter what medication she takes. During painful episodes she subtly lets the other people know. This lets others know that they are not the cause of her discomfort.

4. Keep a high-stakes check list

Keep a check list that you can use before going out. Here's an example which you can adapt yourself:

Item	**Check**
Location	1. Been there before?
	2. Quiet?
	3. Menu—well priced?
	4. Reservation?
	5. Familiar staff?
Clothing	1. Silk, delicate or synthetic?
	2. Shirt—can you breathe freely?
	3. Weather?
Hygiene	1. Antiperspirant?
	2. Perfume?
	3. Gum/mint?

Medical	1. Decongestant?
	2. Anti-allergy?
	3. Inhaler?
	4. Contact lenses?
Tech	1. Phone on silent?

Systemising your life in this way removes external distractions and reduces uncertainty. It stops your body language from corrupting and frees-up brain power so you can focus on projecting charisma through conversation. Managing your internal distractions will put you at an even greater advantage.

5. Leave your phone on silent and in your pocket or handbag

When you are face-to-face with anyone your phone should be out of sight. If an old friend bumps into you on the street while you're writing a long message on WhatsApp, put your phone away without hesitation—you can finish the message later. Also, never place your phone on the table during a conversation even if others do. It may seem harmless to you but it shows a lack of presence.

Chapter 17
Internal Distractions

Being admired and respected largely comes down to managing your own emotions. You only need to look at the effects that certain drugs and alcohol have on the brain. Have you ever knocked back one or two alcoholic drinks and then had a conversation? How much easier is it to express yourself and enjoy the interaction? Don't the opinions and jokes flow so effortlessly? Alcohol acts on GABA receptors in the brain to impair the circuits that make us feel anxious.

What if you could assume a similar level confidence without the influence of alcohol, even if it's only temporary? You can play chemist with your own emotions by adapting your behaviour before and during a social interaction. Before looking at these techniques, it's important that we define and understand the effects of the internal thoughts that prevent us from projecting authority and affection.

Anxiety

Remember Oliver from the coffee shop? Unfortunately, he didn't get the job. To make matters worse, he also failed to convert any of his other interviews. After all this frustration, he came to me for help. Our conversation went something like this:

Me: '*Before we get into the details. Do you have any idea where you're going wrong?'*

Olly: '*Not really. The feedback has been quite vague. I do think my nerves get the better of me sometimes, but everyone gets nervous before interviews, right? Maybe my answers weren't good enough, maybe there are graduates with more work experience? I honestly don't know.'*

Me: '*I doubt it's your CV as it got you the interview in the first place. As for your answers—they were strong. Interviewers hear the same thing every day so what you say isn't as important as how you come across. You mentioned that you were nervous—did this show in the interviews?'*

Olly: *'I definitely wasn't relaxed. I'm always on edge'*

Me: *'When did you start feeling nervous?'*

Olly: *'A few days before the interview and quite a lot on the actual morning'*

Me: *'What made you nervous? What kind of thoughts did you have?'*

Olly: *'I hate being judged, so interviews are very stressful for me. I didn't want to say anything embarrassing. I kept thinking, What if there were more than one interviewer?'*

As Olly was answering my questions I could see that he was working himself up thinking about everything. Clearly he felt a lot of anxiety before and during the interview and it was affecting the way he was coming across. Olly's remarks reveal the first internal distraction that plagues our charisma: social anxiety.

Social Anxiety

Feeling anxious around other people, particularly during 'high-stakes' situations like interviews or public speaking, is completely normal. All of us feel it from time to time. Some more than others.

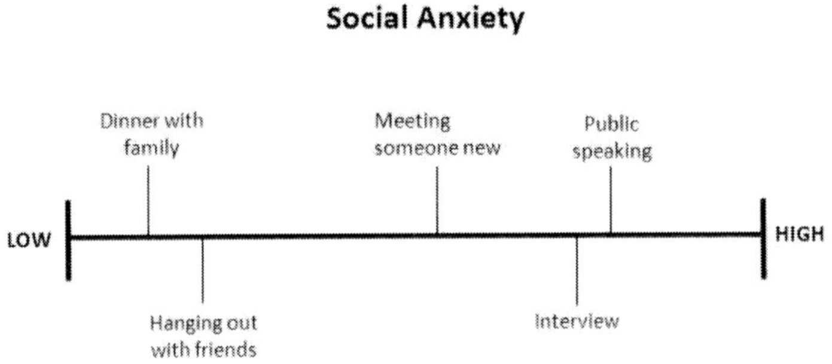

It's important to understand where this anxiety stems from and looking at studies on 'Social Anxiety Disorder' can help us do that. Those with this disorder have an uncontrollable phobia of being embarrassed and judged by others. Imagine the anxiety you felt the last time you were in a 'high-stakes' situation. An individual with this disorder would feel this anxiety almost all the time, even when they're with friends and family.

One of my close friends, Eric, developed severe social anxiety in his early 20s. Conversations with him would be difficult as it took him an abnormally long time to react to anything I said. His eyes were always wide-open like he'd seen a ghost and body language was always awkward. Knowledge of his condition didn't stop me from being uncomfortable around him. When I asked him to describe what was happening in his mind, he said this:

"My anxiety is made up of thoughts like... 'Is my hand in the wrong place? What does Raja think of me? Am I talking too loudly?' These thoughts are constantly running through my head and it almost feels like there is no room for more positive thoughts. My anxiety is sticky gooey gunk running through my brain"

Eric's constant fear of being judged slowed his thoughts down to the point where it became difficult for him to be present in a conversation. In other words, he was so concerned with what other people thought of him, that he barely listened, let alone processed what they were saying. Fortunately, through a special type of therapy called Cognitive Behavioural Therapy or CBT, he learnt how to control his anxiety. This helped (in his own words) 'remove some of the sticky gooey gunk' and allowed him to think faster and process information coherently.

Even though this is an extreme example, it gives you an idea of how much of a distraction social anxiety—and any other anxiety—can be. The stickier your anxious thoughts are, the more anxiety you experience and the harder it is for you to be present during social interactions. Even a thin layer of anxious gunk can affect your body language and ability to think clearly during 'high-stakes' situations. In chapter 18, I'll show you several techniques similar to Cognitive Behavioural Therapy that I used to clear anxiety out of my mind when it was most important. Now back to Oliver.

Olly: *"I got talking to another candidate in the waiting room before the psychometric test. She went to Cambridge, had a lot of big names on her CV and seemed to know a lot more about the industry than me. She mentioned studying a blog post where someone had posted all the questions for the interview. Talking with her really messed with my head"*

Me: *"Because you compared yourself to her?"*

Olly: *"Yeah—I know I shouldn't compare myself to others but I couldn't help it. Sounds pathetic but I convinced myself that she was better than me and I didn't deserve the internship. I assumed the other candidates had similar credentials to her.*

My confidence completely dropped and I became even more nervous before the interview. My heart started racing and I felt like giving up. To make matters worse, I got the interviewer's name wrong when she greeted me!"
Olly had internally 'put down his sword' before even entering the arena just because he believed his opponent had a bigger and better one. This was all too familiar to me.

Insecurity & Self-Doubt

"Who are you kidding? You're just a student. If you can't even do your own washing properly how are you supposed to convince these people to hire and pay you thousands a month?"

"These guys are experienced. They can see right through you!"

These were the type of insecure thoughts that entered my head before high-stakes graduate interviews. People told me that everyone has these nerves, but I never truly believed them until a speaker came into university to give a talk on 'confidence'. She asked:

'Who here thinks they were the one mistake the university admissions team made?

Over half the room put their hands up. I was shocked! How can students with a strong history of academic accomplishments feel like they don't deserve to be where they are? Why do we doubt ourselves so much?

Self-doubt is the lack of confidence and belief in oneself and one's abilities. It is created over time by the suppression of your expression as an individual. When we give our inner critic the chance, it can relentlessly chip away at our confidence.

Some people have a more active critic than others. Many psychologists believe the extent to which we suffer from self-doubt is determined by our past experiences and how much our immediate family focused on failure.

If your parents criticised your failures more than they praised your successes, or you suffered from bullying, it can result in a lack of self-confidence and self-belief down the line. Surprisingly, this happens most often to high academic achievers because they usually have parents who put a ton of pressure on them to succeed. Some of that pressure, either directly or indirectly, comes from emotional blackmail and disapproval.

Those who have a loud inner critic struggle to keep themselves in the top right of the judgement chart. Some show too much authority to compensate for their own warped perceptions of themselves. Others show too little and feel they don't deserve to have authority as they are somehow less than those around them. In reality, no one is better than you and I. It doesn't matter if they are a celebrity or a billionaire, they still shit in a bog and end up in a grave. They might be better actors or business people, but they are not above you and I.

Remember that you are a unique human being with your own identity, principles and talents. There will never be another one of you ever. You only need to be concerned with 'being good at you' and becoming a better version of yourself.

Uncertainty Anxiety

Olly: *'There were so many questions they could ask. I couldn't help but think: What if the interviewers are brutal like the ones on 'The Apprentice'? What if they ask difficult brain teasers? What if I forget what to say?'*

What if?

We all do a great job of simulating the worst possible case scenarios while completely ignoring the best-case ones. This can be useful. Worrying motivates us to solve problems and helps us decide what we should do if our fears materialise. However, do you find yourself running over them again and again?

This happens because we are programmed to like familiarity and feel uncomfortable with uncertainty. Survival is easier when we stick to what we know. If our brains were Twitter, anxiety caused by uncertainty would be the pinned post. Until the outcome is known, anxiety remains pinned to the top of our attention.

Unfortunately, continuously replaying the worst-case scenario can result in a fight or flight response. This is because our brains aren't great at seeing the difference between real and fake. Take horror films for example. We know that it's only a movie with special effects and actors, but our hearts still beat faster when we see the demonic poltergeist appear in the background. That's our fight or flight response and it's triggered by our subconscious believing we're in danger.

We are in no physical danger during a high-stakes event like a job interview, so why do we keep running fearful simulations? At the heart of our worries lie our dreams and aspirations. We value finding a good job and achieving a degree so we feel fear when things that we value are threatened.

As we cycle through the same scenarios over and over again we start to believe it will happen. Adrenaline pumps through our veins and our bodies focus on surviving the next 10 minutes rather than the next 10 years. With all the resulting body language changes, it's not the ideal state to be entering a high-stakes situation in.

Out of all the distractions mentioned, anxiety produced from uncertainty about the future was my biggest problem. Although I managed to keep it in check during university, my biggest breakthrough happened in the first year after university. As a proprietary trader, my job was to take bets on the direction of financial markets like the FTSE 100. When I started taking bets with larger amounts of money, anxiety really started to kick in because predicting if prices were going up or down was very difficult. Every time I bought or sold, a wave of 'what if' scenarios flooded my mind.

What if the market goes down and I lose too much money? What if the risk manager comes over and tells me to go home, how embarrassing would that be? What if they kick me off the graduate program? Even when I wasn't losing money, I continued to recycle these worst-case scenarios. This resulted in premature, incorrect and ultimately unprofitable decisions.

This habit affected other areas of my life as well. I was uncomfortable with silences during important conversations and blurted out information I shouldn't, all because I wasn't sure what the other person was thinking.

With my trading account losing money and pressure mounting, I launched an all-out attack on my anxiety. When I started paying attention to my thoughts and consciously using techniques to handle them, my anxiety decreased and I started performing better in many different aspects of my life. Handling internal distractions at university was one thing, but handling day-to-day anxieties brought on by my career fell well outside my comfort zone. Fortunately, I found effective ways to control my anxieties and that is what I'll discuss in the next chapter.

Internal Distractions

Social anxiety, uncertainty anxiety, self-doubt—how can we prevent these from affecting us? The only way is to remove yourself from modern society, to go live in a monastery and meditate for several years.

These feelings are deeply rooted in our psyche and will appear even when we try our best to prevent them. There is no easy or quick way to get rid of them completely. However, we can learn to manage them in such a way that they don't have a big impact. Doing this better than your peers will give you a big edge with regards to your c-skills and other areas of your life. This requires both proactive and reactive effort.

Feeling anxious is not always a bad thing. Sometimes you need a little underlying self-doubt to keep you working and pushing to be better. For example, when there is a real problem in your life like finishing university with 27k in debt and no job, being anxious is good. You'll work to solve that problem in order to alleviate the anxiety. As long as your anxiety is not disproportionately out of line and distracting you every few minutes, it can help you to succeed.

However, when it comes to high-stakes situations like interviews or public speaking, we need to be confident and can't let anxiety distract us.

I'm always a little paranoid and insecure in the weeks and days running up to a high-stakes situation, but on the day I take steps to temporarily increase my confidence. Steps which you'll soon discover are a little unorthodox.

Think of your mind as a pendulum. We want the pendulum to be stable and not swinging all over the place. In this stable state, our emotions are in control and we can make better rational decisions. We can see the world as it actually is rather than the skewed version our mind simulates. But this is easier said than done, because when you get criticised by your tutor or enter a room full of strangers, your pendulum starts swinging.

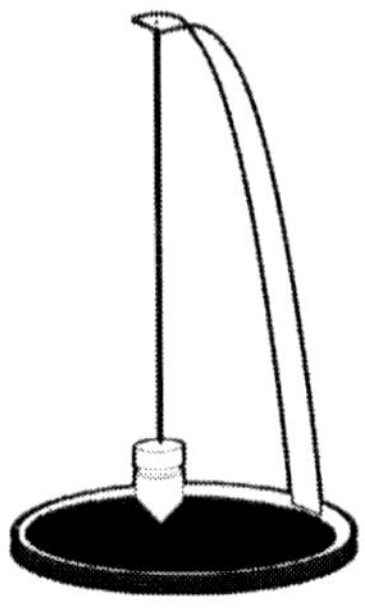

It's important that we learn how to keep the pendulum in our brain as stable as possible. We do this by:

1. Making it heavy and difficult to move (proactive efforts)
2. Knocking it back when it's out of place (reactive efforts)

Chapter 18
What is the Anxiety Cycle?

The different anxieties discussed in the previous chapter are fuelled by a cycle of thoughts, feelings, physical reactions and behaviours.

The cycle starts with a thought. Think back to when Oliver spoke to the other candidate before his interview. His initial thought was 'this candidate is more qualified than me'. This led to a feeling of insecurity and an increased heart rate (physical reaction). Forgetting the interviewer's name was a behavioural change because Olly wouldn't make that mistake under normal circumstances.

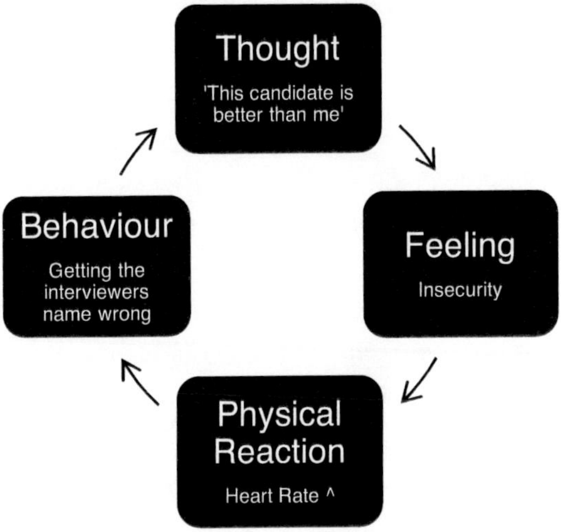

All four stages of the anxiety cycle are closely related. Making changes to one can cause changes in others. If you can change your way of thinking, your behaviour and feelings will change; if you can change your behaviour, your thoughts and feelings will change too. Tackling all of them together can choke anxiety and stop it from taking hold. By the end of this chapter, that is exactly what you'll learn to do.

Starting with your thoughts, we'll move through each part of the cycle. I'll describe techniques and provide exercises to help you tackle each element.

Thoughts

Olly: "I should never have spoken to that girl. She triggered my anxious thoughts"

Me: *"Yes, she did, but even if you didn't speak to her there's a good chance something else would have triggered them. You could have seen a painting on the wall that reminded you of GCSE art, which lead to a thought about how you failed it, which then reminded you of every failure you've had—and then, low and behold, you're stuck in the anxious cycle again"*

We can't avoid the triggers that cause an anxious thought because they're everywhere. The thought is coming whether you like it or not. What about ignoring the thought altogether? Well, that's easier said than done. If I ask you to *not* think of a big red bus, what do you think of?

Studies on this phenomena show that the longer candidates suppress the thought, the more viciously it comes back and the longer it remains. So, if avoiding triggers or ignoring a thought is pointless, how can we get rid of our anxiety and be our most charismatic self? The most effective option is to manage the thought using a methodology like Cognitive Behavioural Therapy (CBT).

As I mentioned earlier, CBT is used by psychiatrists to disrupt damaging thought patterns in those who suffer from severe and frequent anxiety. It has grown in popularity over the past three decades due to positive results backed by strong scientific evidence.

"It seems that CBT can change your brain and rewire it"

- Dr Paul Blenkiron, Consultant Psychiatrist

These benefits are by no means exclusive to extreme sufferers. Anyone, including those who experience normal short-term anxiety, can benefit too.

When learning about CBT at university, I found the books very longwinded and difficult to follow. For this reason, I created a similar but simplified methodology which proved to be very effective. Over time I've refined these techniques, particularly in the first few years in my career as a trader. During this time, I consulted with psychologists and CBT specialists to improve my performance at work. Based on their guidance, advancements in the field of CBT and my own research, I built upon the techniques I used at university to create the Acknowledge, Neutralise & Transform strategy or ANT for short.

Chapter 19
ANT

ANT takes the core principles of CBT and turns them into actionable mental exercises you can do anytime negative thoughts appear. These exercises helped me a lot during university and even more so during the first few years of my anxiety-filled career. They are second nature to me now. Take the time to understand them, don't be lazy about using them and they will help you too!

Step 1: Acknowledge

Most of the time we think without knowing we're thinking. Random thoughts enter and leave our consciousness. To manage these thoughts, we need to stop being the 'thinker' and start being the 'observer'. Next time any fears of failure or embarrassment enter your mind:

1. Collect the thought and give it an identity or name. Refer to the thought as *he* or *she* and *they.*

2. Pretend you're observing your mind and the thoughts running through it as if you're a separate entity—a scientist assessing the situation.

3. Belittle the thought with sarcasm and humour.

Typically, the same anxious thoughts or 'culprits' appear again and again. One my culprits at uni was the fear that I'd embarrass myself in front of the class during presentations. This fear popped into my head at random moments in the days running up to the assessment day and the minutes or seconds before giving my presentation. This was more or less my audit trail before delivering the presentation:

00:00:01 I'm feeling tired
00:00:02 Shouldn't have gone out yesterday; should have slept earlier
00:00:03 Maybe more breakfast could have helped
00:00:04 Why did that hot girl have to sit in the front row?
00:00:05 Look how many people there are!
00:00:06 I really can't get a bad grade
00:00:07 I'm going to flop and embarrass myself
00:00:08 I hope I don't go first
00:00:09 Fear anxiety again—he's back again! **(Acknowledge)**

Simply acknowledging an anxious thought interrupts your audit trail and reduces the chance of further anxiety. Detaching yourself from your thoughts also helps you to become a little more objective. If you're still feeling anxious and can't help other negative thoughts making their way in, it's time to neutralise.

Step 2: Neutralise

The brain is a well-designed organ, but it's not perfect. It can interpret situations incorrectly and make poor assumptions. We blow small problems and mistakes out of proportion and think that consequences are far worse than they actually are. Here are some of the cognitive habits we fall into:

Cognitive Habits	**Description**	**Example**
Generalising	Making too much of a situation.	If you receive a bad grade in a test, you assume you are terrible at that subject.
Labelling	Calling yourself names.	One bad grade and you call yourself 'stupid'. A wrong word in a conversation and you're 'idiotic'.
Filtering	Focusing on problems and weaknesses while disregarding strengths and accomplishments.	You receive a marked essay from your tutor and she provides 10 compliments and 1 criticism. All you think about is the criticism.

Black & White Thinking	Either something is really good or really bad. There is no in-between.	If something isn't spectacular, then by default it's awful.
Fortune telling	Simulating what could happen in the future and then responding emotionally if these are actually going to happen.	Oliver thinking about the interviewer being interrogative like Alan Sugar. The interviewer is there to help you, understands you are a graduate and has no intention of humiliating you.

These cognitive habits become more intense when we're in an anxious state because we start noticing pieces of evidence that reaffirm our anxiety. For example, if you consider yourself uninteresting and someone keeps breaking eye contact, you'll assume that you're being boring when you're not. The actual reason for their behaviour could be anything from their own internal distraction to a quiet burp they don't want you to know about!

By being aware of your own cognitive habits and understanding when you're viewing the world through a 'negative lens', you'll give yourself and others the benefit of the doubt. You'll also learn to trust your ability to read situations and other people. Of course, this comes with practice, but also from continuously questioning and neutralising your negative thoughts. Next time you acknowledge an anxious thought:

1. Remind yourself that 'a thought is not a fact'.

2. Think about what you would say to a friend who came to you with the same anxious thought.

3. Think what a friend would tell you if you told them your thought.

Back to the example of my uni presentation, this would by the audit trail in my mind if I continued to feel anxious after acknowledging my thoughts:

00:00:06 I really can't get a bad grade
00:00:07 I'm going to flop and embarrass myself
00:00:08 I hope I don't go first
00:00:09 Fear anxiety again—he's back again! **(Acknowledge)**
00:00:10 You're not real—just a simulation **(Neutralise)**

Now it's time to transform!

Step 3: Transform

By changing your interpretation of a negative thought and putting a positive spin on it, you can dampen anxiety and find the silver lining, wherever it may be. Say it out loud or write it down.

Take Oliver's interview day experience as an example. His negative thought was, 'I'm not good enough and don't deserve this internship'. This can be spun into, 'Well, actually I got this far so they must think I'm good enough' or 'I must be good if I'm competing with a Cambridge graduate of this calibre'.

*Four people go outside and step in dog mess. The first, who is depressed, thinks 'There you go, I'm useless, I can't do anything right and I may as well go back to bed'. This person feels sad and low. The second who is anxious thinks, 'Oh no, I've stepped in dog mess. I will need to change. What if I'm late for work? What if I'm fired?' This person feels highly anxious. The third, who has problems with anger, thinks, 'if I find the b**?!d that let his dog s*** on my doorstep I will beat him up so badly that he'll never walk another b**?!y dog again.' This person feels angry. However, the fourth, who has had CBT (or ANT), thinks, 'Well at least I remembered to put on my shoes.' This person feels pleased.*

- Professor Paul Salkovskis

Your consciousness is remarkably malleable. Sad thoughts make you feel sad. Happy thoughts make you feel happy. You burn your toast? Great—less carbs. You sleep through your alarm? Great—more sleep. You embarrassed yourself? At least you have a funny story to tell. If being conveniently deluded helps you deflate internal distractions caused by irrational anxiety, then so be it!

Another way to change your interpretation of a negative thought, is by adding perspective. I constantly remind myself of my own mortality:

'I could die tomorrow'
'My mum, dad or girlfriend could die tomorrow'

Although morbid, briefly thinking of a loved one passing away provides immediate perspective and reveals how insignificant your anxiety is. Reminding yourself that you're not alone also achieves the same affect. Billions of people around the world experience anxious thoughts every day so you're not broken just because you feel sad or insecure. Think about that for a second. You are one of 7.6 billion people in the world who are more or less wired the same way. Think about how small you are relative to your city, country, continent, planet, solar system, galaxy and universe. Think about how many people are facing serious illness, injury, bereavement and poverty; how many people are literally in a life or death situation at the very same moment that you're worried about an exam or an interview.

Doesn't the problem seem a little smaller now? After acknowledging and neutralising a negative thought, transform it by:

1. Finding the silver lining and using it to reframe the negative thought into a positive one.
2. Thinking about your own or a loved one's mortality.

3. Looking at the bigger picture and realising that you're an insignificant speck and your issue is even less significant.
4. Remembering that you're only one person out of billions trying to manage their own fears and concerns.

ANT: Acknowledge, Neutralise & Transform

Ultimately, any anxiety, negative thought or insecurity is nothing more than a thought. Just as it begins with a thought it can also end with a thought. Understanding your own psychology can help you when the going gets tough.

Internal distractions are like mosquitos that keep coming back to bite. You need to consciously and proactively swat them down using ANT. Doing so will help you to manage anxiety, improve your body language and give you an edge over the Cambridge graduate sitting next to you in the waiting room.

Step 1 – Acknowledge – *'oh you again'*

Step 2 – Neutralise – *'you're not real'*

Step 3 – Transform – *'I could die tomorrow'*

Now that you know how to tackle your thoughts, we can discuss ways to adapt your feelings and physical reactions.

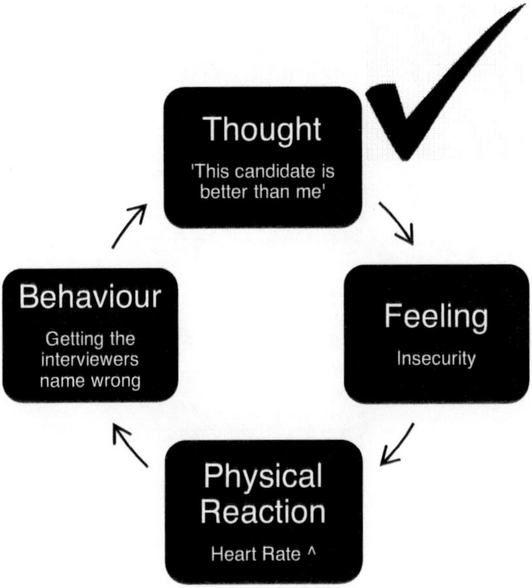
Thought
'This candidate is better than me'
Feeling
Insecurity
Physical Reaction
Heart Rate ^
Behaviour
Getting the interviewers name wrong

Chapter 20

Alter your Feelings using Biological Loopholes

Changing our thoughts requires a conscious effort; altering our feelings and emotions requires some knowledge of biology. There are two hormones involved in adapting our feelings to ensure we display authority and affection. These are Testosterone, which is known as the 'Dominance Hormone', and Cortisol, the 'Stress Hormone'. Higher amounts of testosterone in your blood lead to more confident, assertive and dominant body language. Higher levels of cortisol indicate stress and discomfort.

These two hormones appear time and time again in studies that compare authoritative and powerful individuals to those who are submissive. In a study done on chimpanzee hierarchies, alpha-males had higher levels of testosterone and lower levels of cortisol in their blood. Similar results have been seen with powerful and effective leaders. Good leaders tend to be confident, are able to take risks and are unaffected by short-term stress. After all, what use is a leader who's dominant when times are good, but falls apart when the going gets tough?

Studies have also shown that testosterone levels spike and cortisol levels fall when an individual needs to take over a leadership role. So, there is plenty of evidence to show the connection between these two hormones and authoritative behaviour.

It's these hormones that we need to influence and, luckily, this isn't as difficult as it sounds. Two loopholes in our physiology enable us to fool the biological systems that control these hormones.

Loophole 1: Specific poses and body language directly affects hormone levels.

Loophole 2: The endocrine system that controls hormones is unable to differentiate between reality and imagination.

The following sections will describe two techniques you can use to exploit these loopholes and essentially play chemist with your own body. Both techniques are backed by strong science so be prepared to be amazed!

Power Poses

In chapter 6, I showed you how closely linked our body and mind is and how our body language mirrors our internal state without us even knowing. What if I was to tell you that the reverse is also true and your body language can influence your internal feelings?

The idea that body language can affect physiology has been around for a while. You may have heard advice like, 'Smile when you're down and it will make you feel better'. A quick way to test this theory is by putting a pen in your mouth so that you contract the smile muscles. Try it now and think of the most depressing memory that comes to mind. Is it difficult?

Very little was discussed about this topic until the American social scientist, Amy Cuddy, took YouTube by storm with her TED talk: 'Your body language shapes who you are'. In the 20-minute talk, she described a lab controlled experiment that she conducted to test whether body language affected physiology.

Forty-two participants were asked to provide saliva samples and assume high-power and low-power poses.

High-power poses:

Low-power poses:

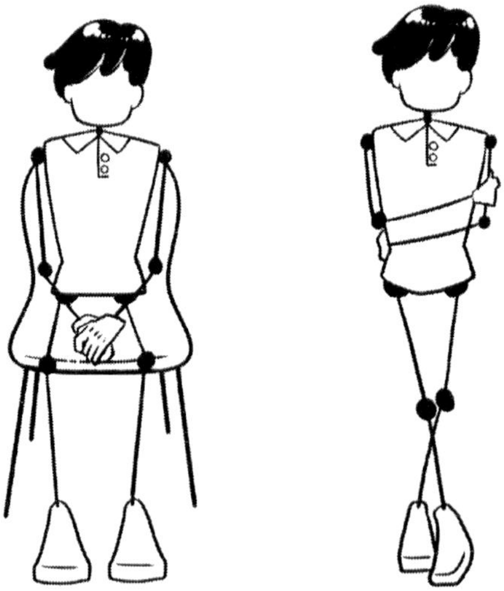

All candidates were left alone in a room and held either two high-power poses or two low-power poses for 1 minute each. They were then asked to participate in a gambling task which tested their risk tolerance and asked how 'powerful' and 'in charge' they felt on a scale from 1 (not at all) to 4 (a lot). Seventeen minutes later a second saliva sample was taken from each participant and the results were astonishing.

Risk tolerance levels shifted significantly. 86% of those who assumed the high-power pose chose the riskier option in the gambling game. Only 60% of the low-power pose candidates chose the same way.

Feelings changed. High-power posers reported feeling significantly more "powerful" and "in charge" (average score of 2.57 out of 4) than low-power posers did (average score of 1.83 out of 4).

Testosterone levels changed. The candidate's testosterone levels increased by 20% after a high-power pose, while dropping by 10% for a low-power pose.

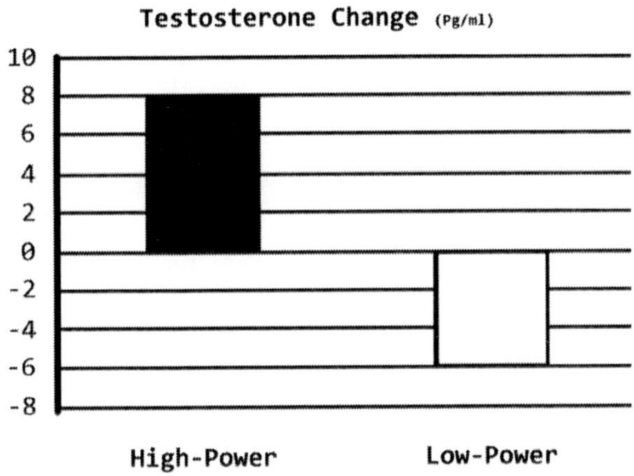

Cortisol levels changed. The high-power group experienced a 25-percent decrease in the hormone, while the low-power group experienced a 15-percent increase.

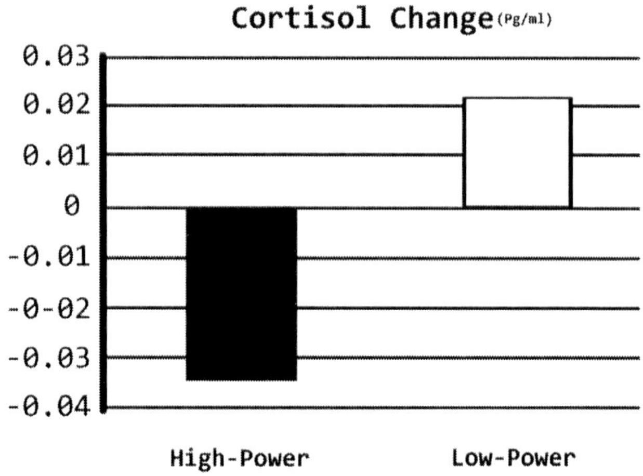

All these physiological and psychological changes occurred from just 2-minutes of posing! Amy's results not only proved that high-power poses induce a positive response in our bodies, but that low-power poses induce a negative response. She also proved that not only do our feelings affect our body language, but our body language also affects our feelings.

Ever since Amy's talk, I have religiously power-posed before any high-stakes situation, including my own TEDx talk! Not only did I feel more confident, but many individuals who watched my talk made similar observations. Based on the strong evidence and my own improvement, I now advise all my mentees and students to use these poses before entering high-stakes situations. Here are the other ones recommended by Amy:

Have an interview, networking event or a date coming up? Arrive five minutes early, head into a private area or toilet cubicle and hold two of the above poses for 2 minutes each.

Success Compilation

Visualisation can provide similar benefits to power-posing. This is a common technique used by professional athletes that involves vividly imagining winning a high-stakes game or tournament. The benefits of this are well documented.

Certain types of audio can also help. Listening to music and even singing have resulted in lower cortisol levels in a range of studies.

And what about video? We know horror movies can fool our minds into thinking we're in danger and studies have shown cortisol levels increase when watching these types of movies. Is there any other evidence?

Much like the experiment Amy Cuddy conducted, another American scientist, Prof Oliver Schultheiss of the University of Michigan, proved that not only do movies alter our hormone levels, but the types of movies can cause profoundly different hormonal reactions.

He took a bunch of participants, split them into three groups and measured their hormone levels before and after watching parts of a movie. One group watched a few scenes from The Godfather Part II. The second group watched one from The Bridges of Madison County and a third watched a documentary on the Amazon rainforest.

The rainforest group recorded no change in hormone levels. Interestingly, the Bridges of Madison County, with a female lead and more of a chick-flick, left women's testosterone levels unchanged, but made those of men drop. Men and women also reacted differently to a Godfather scene in which Vito Corleone acquires power after killing a foe.

High-testosterone men saw their testosterone levels soar by as much as 30 per cent; high-testosterone women saw their testosterone fall. This was perhaps because The Godfather is about males fighting males.

From the results of this study, we can conclude that:

1. Men relate to other men and women to other women from a hormonal perspective.

2. Each sex responds positively to their counterpart 'winning' or being dominant and negatively to 'losing' or submissiveness.

3. Although controls for both Cuddy and Schultheiss studies were different, testosterone levels increased more in response to video compared with power posing.

It's clear that watching or even visualising powerful imagery, which promotes the release of testosterone and retraction of cortisol, helps us to project authority.

Visualising or watching people we relate to in a winning scenario creates a positive mental and physiological response. Therefore, watching or thinking about ourselves winning will create the strongest and most favourable response. After all, we relate to ourselves more than anyone else.

Three years ago I uploaded a few pictures of proud moments from my life onto my phone. My goal was to build a collection of memories that I could look at if I needed a boost of testosterone and a drop in cortisol. Before a high-stake situation at work, I glanced through the photos and it worked incredibly well.

After fishing through Facebook, old hard-drives and phones, this small collection of photos eventually evolved into a full-blown video compilation lasting just over two minutes. It contained clips of me posing with my results on A-level results day, highlights of my graduation, my reaction when offered my summer internship, before & after shots from a fitness program, and a Champagne cork I kept from my most profitable trading day. I've probably watched this video a hundred times and it has had a big impact. I don't hesitate to stick my headphones in and watch it whenever I need my A-game.

The success compilation continues to grow. Recently, I added clips from my TEDx talk and a snapchat video a friend took at a celebratory night out after sales for my book How to ACE Your A-levels/GCSE passed the 10,000 mark.

After sharing this idea with students, many have experienced similar positive effects and improvements. One student who shared the idea with her family received a surprise Success Compilation video made by her dad on the morning of a graduate assessment centre and interview. In her words:

'I had to fix my mascara as it made me cry a little in the beginning! But the memories, music and the motivational message from my parents and sisters at the end helped me feel really confident. My nerves were gone! I'm pretty sure I was

the best performer in the group exercise and I think the interviewer liked me!'

She was invited back for a final round interview, used the video again and received the internship offer the very next day.

How to Create a Success Compilation

1. Collect old photo and video content including clips of.

    a. Yourself: Look for proud moments where you displayed powerful body language and confidence.

    b. People you Admire: These could be historic political figures, celebrities or your mentor.

    c. Friends & Family: Include a few clips of your favourites and those who you want to make proud.

2. Use video editing software to compile the content and add an audio track or voiceover.

    a. I've found iMovies on the Apple App Store the easiest and most intuitive editing software to use. If you don't have time to do it yourself, send the content to a freelancer on Fiverr.com or PeoplePerHour.com and it shouldn't cost you more than £30.

3. Add powerful and inspiring music.

    a. Start with a Hans Zimmer type movie soundtrack preferably from a memorable scene filled with power and inspiration. Gladiator, Lord of the Rings, Hunger Games—you choose.

    b. You can also record and add a message to yourself or have someone you admire record one for you.

4. Start filming! We capture almost everything on our phones these days, so just shift the focus to proud moments and don't be afraid to make it all about you. When important coursework marks are coming out, keep your phone ready to capture the moment. Get your friends & family involved and try to record genuine emotionally powerful reactions.

    a. Be sure to add clips. My goal is to have an hour-long compilation I can watch when I'm lying prone in a nursing home with tubes up my nose!

5. Stick your headphones in and watch the video before any high-stakes situation.

After explaining the procedure to students, the number one question I'm asked is:

"Don't you feel silly sitting on the toilet with your headphones on watching a video of yourself?"

Of course I do. However, those who succeed always go the extra mile regardless of how silly they feel. If we're up against 200 of our peers presenting a thesis or 50 other candidates for the same job we need to do something different. This is a game of small margins. That extra bit of confidence from that extra bit of testosterone might provide the edge needed to surpass everyone else. If you want it enough, it stops being silly and becomes necessary.

Furthermore, technology is continuously improving various areas of our lives from how we get from place to place (Uber) to how we connect (Facebook). We have the advantage of being able to carry around and use technology anywhere, so I see no reason why we can't use it to help us perform in high-stakes situation and give a boost to our c-skills.

Now that you know how power posing and a Success Compilation can influence your feelings, I want to show you two techniques that can help control physical reactions as a result of particularly high anxiety situations.

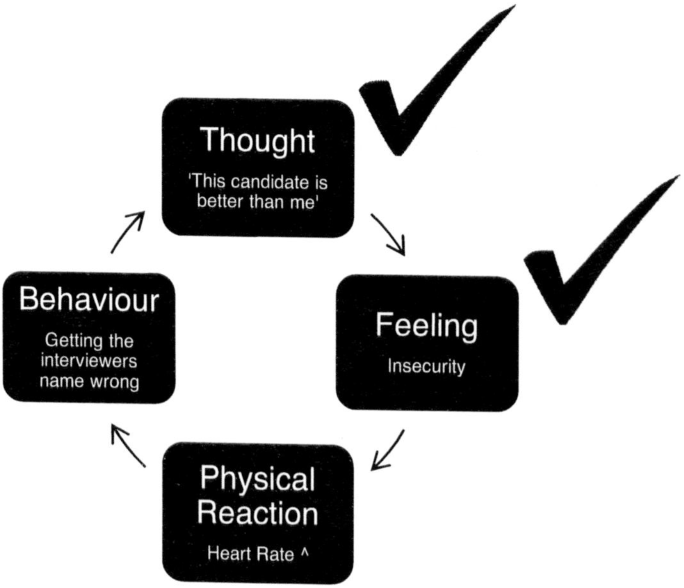
Thought
'This candidate is better than me'
Feeling
Insecurity
Physical Reaction
Heart Rate ^
Behaviour
Getting the interviewers name wrong

Chapter 21
Physical Reactions

At a talk in Portsmouth, a well-known neuroscientist called Dr Allan Watkins did a demonstration on stage to show how a person reacts to challenge. He took a volunteer from the audience and hooked them up to a heart-rate monitor. As explained to the audience that he was about to give him a mathematical challenge, his heart-rate shot up to 90. It settled back down but shot up again when he began asking maths questions, deliberately pressuring him by telling him his answers were wrong even when they weren't. His heart-rate continued to increase and the psychological effects of the subject became apparent as he stuttered and fumbled.

As physiological effects from anxiety appear, the pre-frontal cortex of the brain becomes deprived. It changes the quality of your thoughts and the thoughts themselves. This is why we blurt out stupid things when we're nervous and why Oliver got the interviewer's name wrong!

This is why we need to keep an eye on our physiology, particularly in the early stages of a high-stakes situation. We want to think as clearly as possible until we hit our stride in the conversational tennis match.

Face Splash

In the movie 8-mile, Rabbit (Eminem) is about to go on stage to 'battle' in front of a crowd who won't hesitate to shame him if he messes up. In the movie soundtrack 'Lose Yourself' he briefly rapped about the physical reactions he experienced before going on stage:

"His palms are sweaty, knees weak, arms are heavy, he's nervous"

In preparation to go on stage, he goes to the bathroom and takes a sip of water. We also see this in other movies all the time where the character either takes a sip of or splashes their face with cold water to calm their nerves. Where did this habit come from and does it actually help?

Yes, it does, and there is proof!

Splashing cold water on our face kicks in the 'mammalian diving response', a phenomenon that occurs when something cold or wet touches our skin. It prepares us for survival under water and slows our heart-rate down to prepare for imminent low oxygen levels. This is why you can hold your breath longer underwater than on ground.

Next time you experience strong physical reactions to anxiety, splash your face with water three times. Lowering your heart-rate will have a knock-on effect on any other physical reactions and help you feel calmer.

We've now discussed how the ANT technique can help you deal with negative thoughts. Learned how power-posing and a Success Compilation improves your feelings and why a simple face-splash can improve your physical symptoms. Now we can tackle the last element of the anxiety cycle: 'behaviour'.

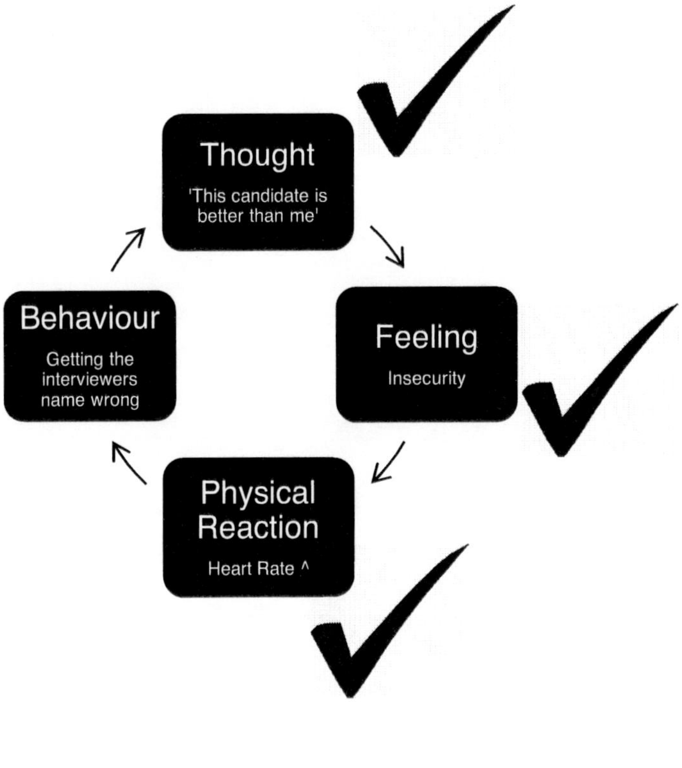

Chapter 22
How Changing Your Behaviour can Strangle Anxiety

At university I met an individual called Matteus who had an interesting hobby. He was a 'pickup artist'; a term used to describe individuals (mostly men) who use techniques to seduce the opposite sex. Matteus often uploads videos of himself getting girls' phone numbers on high streets and in bars. He is extremely charismatic.

Matteus wasn't always this good, though. In fact, he used to be quite shy and suffered from extreme (in his own words) 'approach anxiety'. When spotting someone he was attracted to, nervousness would take over and stop him from even saying 'hello'. Naturally I was interested in how he conquered his anxiety, so I asked him and he told me:

"One day I became so sick of being scared of rejection that I decided to get rejected 100 times"

Matteus then explained how he continuously spoke to women on public transport, on the street, bars and clubs with the sole purpose of being rejected! He kept a tally of the number of rejections he received and stopped when it got to 100. This crazy task kickstarted a period of exponential improvement.

"It's not that I didn't feel the anxiety anymore, I just became less sensitive to it and did a better job of ignoring it. Think about it: What's the best way of getting into a cold swimming pool? Tread in one step at a time or just jump? What's the best way of removing a plaster? Slowly peeling it or ripping it quickly? The first options require more willpower initially but get you to the end goal faster"

Matteus didn't step out of his comfort zone, he leapt out of it. Rather than facing his fear he punched it in the face. By getting rejected so many times he found a way to become comfortable with discomfort. His story inspired me to reduce the anxiety I felt before interviews with senior professionals.

Selling yourself to a girl or guy you fancy is not too different from selling yourself to an interviewer or anyone else you meet. In the summer before my third year, I vowed to desensitise myself to anxiety by approaching 100 senior professionals.

My way of punching fear was to speak with as many senior professionals and interviewers as possible. I did this by first applying to several companies and signing up to multiple networking events.

These events were designed to educate graduates about the different roles available to them. They typically began with a talk followed by a networking session where you could speak to employees at the company.

I'd often skip the networking part because I found it uncomfortable. I couldn't be bothered to queue or join the huddle around company employees and worried about asking a stupid question. My worry was that they'd somehow remember me and it would reduce my chances of getting the job—irrational, I know. Anyway, this time around, I pushed myself to speak to as many people as possible even if it meant being the last person to leave the event. Three months later my tally hit 100, my confidence skyrocketed and I started building momentum.

At an interview skills workshop hosted by the UCL economics society, a somewhat stern and intimidating host asked a volunteer to come up on stage in front of 60 people and to conduct a 'live interview'. No one put their hand up for at least 30 seconds, even when the host and society organisers tried to encourage one of us to. During this time, I was going back and forth thinking about whether to volunteer or not. If it had been the year before, I would have pretended to write something down in my notes and prayed they didn't randomly choose me. However, the story of Matteus's 100 rejections was echoing in my head so after mumbling: 'Screw it,' I put my hand up and walked to the stage.

Answering the first question he asked was a little nerve-racking and I fumbled a little. It drew a short giggle from the audience.

However, the rest of the interview went really well and I felt really relieved after finishing it. If I could handle an interview in front of 60+ people judging me, surely I could handle one senior professional. This was a real turning point. Whenever I felt anxious before meeting an interviewer or senior professional, I would remind myself of the 'live interview' on stage.

Continuously leaping outside your comfort zone in low-stakes scenarios can deposit some proud moments in your memory bank. These are powerful tools you can call upon when anxiety inevitably comes knocking. In our 6-Month Charisma Project, I'll set you a task called '20 Days of Rejection' which you can do on your own or with a friend. Each day you will complete a dare that will desensitise you to fear and choke your anxieties.

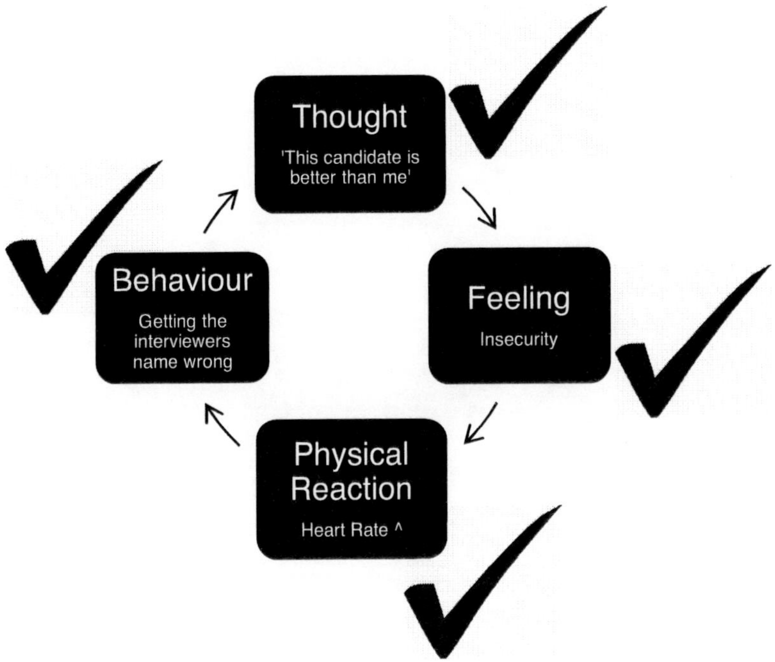
Thought
'This candidate is better than me'
Feeling
Insecurity
Physical Reaction
Heart Rate ^
Behaviour
Getting the interviewers name wrong

Chapter 23
Stabilising the Pendulum

After sharing my techniques with Oliver, he was eager to start using them for his next interview in 3 weeks. He didn't have enough time to complete my Charisma Project so I gave him a shortened version.

First, he created a Success Compilation, then I helped him build a checklist geared towards dragging him out of his comfort zone in the lead-up to the interview.

The checklist looked a little something like this:

1. Increase the number of people you interact with 3-fold.

2. Ask every newsagent, receptionist and cleaning staff how their day is going.

3. Stand opposite to everyone else in the elevator and pay close attention to your discomfort.

4. Schedule at least 3 mock interviews with the university careers service.

5. Attend 2 society events where you don't know anyone and go there alone.

6. Attend 3 company open evenings and start conversations with the most senior looking employees.

At first, Olly found some of the tasks quite uncomfortable, particularly attending the society events alone. Nevertheless, he pushed through and improved significantly.

On the night before the interview, he prepared his suit and picked a shirt that didn't restrict his breathing. He completed 10 minutes of meditation and 10 minutes of visualisation before sleeping, and then he repeated this immediately upon waking.

He was ready to go, but as soon as he began his journey to the interview, the anxiety kicked in. Memories of past failures and negative thoughts became more frequent, and he began to doubt himself. But having trained in ANT, he knew how to strike these doubts down every time they entered his head.

He left his halls an hour early to avoid any unexpected delays, but unfortunately his train was delayed by 20 minutes. This began the first strong negative thoughts. He feared being late to the interview, considered calling ahead and thought about what he would say. He decided to use the train delay to strike up a conversation with another annoyed commuter.

Turning to a woman next to him he said, "So annoying isn't it!? I've got an interview to get to!" She responded sympathetically and shared her concerns about getting to work on time. They had a short exchange and then stepped onto the train. The conversation immediately relaxed Oliver, knowing that someone else was in the same boat as him; and leaping out of his comfort zone by talking with a stranger also got his social juices flowing.

After a few changes, he arrived at his final train station and found a coffee shop near the company offices. He made eye contact and smiled at the barista as he ordered some tea, just as he'd done to the Network Rail staff and many other commuters he'd passed on his journey.

He sat down and read through his interview notes to jog his memory. There were certain parts he forgot and this drew the inevitable anxious thoughts, 'What if I forget my examples or my answers and freeze up?' The thoughts distracted him and took him on an anxious tangent which stopped him from reading through the rest of his notes. Olly used ANT again:

Acknowledge: The thought started with, 'What if...' so he diagnosed himself with the fear of uncertainty and smiled a little as he remembered how predictable anxious thoughts are.

Neutralise: Olly reminded himself about why our minds simulate the worst-case scenario even when the chances of it happening are low. 'A thought is not a fact'.

Transform: 'OK—so I forget an example, can't blag myself out of it and freeze up (which I've never done) then what? It's only one question and I'm a graduate, not a seasoned professional. The interviewer isn't going to penalise me for that. Even if they do and I don't get the offer—so what? What doesn't kill me only makes me stronger. I'll step up my game in the next interview and be even more prepared than I was for this one'.

Spinning his thought into a positive got his head back on track and he finished reading through his notes. With twenty minutes left until the interview, he left the coffee shop and walked to the company offices.

After finding his way to the 14th floor, and with fifteen minutes to spare, Olly found an empty cubicle in the men's toilets. He closed his eyes, controlled his breathing, visualised himself in the interview and proceeded to strike three high-power poses for two minutes a pose. He then took a seat, pulled out his phone and watched his success compilation.

Pumped up, he was ready for the interview!

Olly went straight to the waiting room where he smiled and spoke to several of the other interviewees for a few minutes, before being called to the interview room. His first few exchanges with the interviewer went perfectly. For the first time, Olly trusted himself to handle any question that came his way and felt confident the moment he sat down.

Olly converted the interview into a second-round assessment centre and eventually an internship offer. He had doubts about himself just like the rest of us, but he proactively took steps towards squeezing the anxiety cycle to allow his personality to shine.

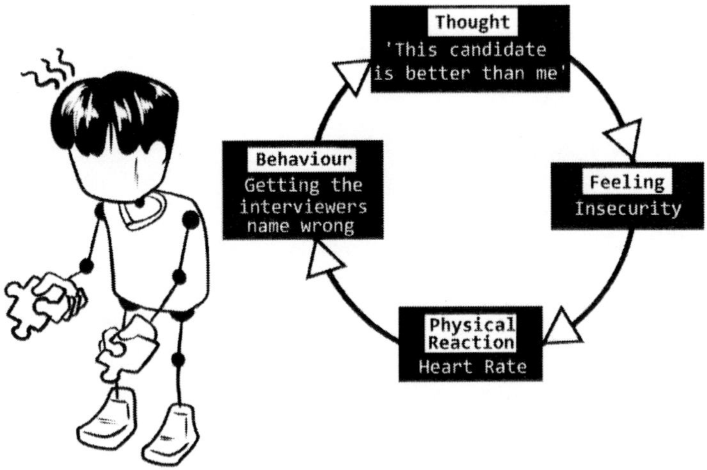

Charismatic people are articulate, witty and creative with their words. Even in a short conversation, you'll need to generate hundreds of conversational ideas and choose from multiple pathways. We need to process information quickly to select the best words and make correct decisions. Managing your external and internal distractions, in the way I described, will give you this speed and enable your conscious mind to do what it does best. Project dominant body language and mesmerise people with your words.

Verbal & Body Language Secrets

Chapter 24
Body Language Simplified

In a study conducted by MIT, candidates were asked to watch a video of various sales pitches from a number of people without sound. They were able to predict the success of each sales pitch with 80% accuracy from only looking at body language.

Life's a pitch and body language helps you sell yourself and your ideas.

There is a lot of information available on this subject and it's very easy to fall into 'information paralysis'. In my opinion, there's no point reading a 300-page book on body language because executing all that advice will be a nightmare. Knowing what good and bad body language looks like and practicing the core two ideas—eye contact and space consumption—is all you need to remember.

Eye Contact

If we're talking about eye contact, then we don't need to look any further than Russell Brand. He is an eye contact specialist! By looking deeply into people's eyes for extended periods of time he sometimes initially makes them feel uncomfortable. Then, after a little while, it completely disarms them. The right-wing extremists and politicians he has gone toe-to-toe with have had no chance because of his lengthy gaze.

Watch any video of Russell and you'll see exactly what I mean. It even works in our slightly reserved British culture. Extended eye contact is one of the few good body language habits that transcends most borders and cultures. This is why I place it at the top of my priority list and why you should too.

As a rule of thumb, more eye contact is better than less. Looking into another person's eyes can produce a deeper connection than physical contact. If you find this difficult to do, looking at the nose is the next best thing as they won't be able to tell the difference.

Also, many find it easier to maintain eye contact while listening than talking. So, get your eyes back where they should be even when it feels uncomfortable. Doing so will immediately raise your social value with the person(s) you are talking to.

Space Consumption

As we touched upon briefly when talking about power-posing, many animals make themselves bigger to display authority. Chimpanzees, for example, pump their chests and swing their arms. Many bird species blow air into their throats and expand their chests.

Humans are no different. We instinctively show respect to those who move their bodies or pose in a spatially greedy way. One study done on business leaders showed that most cross their legs when they sit, which tends to use up more space. Other studies have showed that men who use large gestures in bars are more attractive to women.

In a social gathering—such as a student night or networking event—where you may want to meet new people, using large gestures and claiming the space around you is key. This is particularly true if you are at the gathering for a long period of time. Your body language not only influences the people you're speaking to but also those catching glimpses of you from a distance. They're looking for the key influencers in the room, so show them you're one of them.

Some of my mentees don't feel comfortable using this type of body language. They say, 'I can't walk like that—everyone will think I'm a pompous prick'. Record yourself walking with your shoulders back, head taught or sitting with your arms spread out and judge for yourself. You won't look as awkward as you think.

There is obviously a line, and if you are slouching back on your chair with your legs wide open and arms spread like an airplane, you've probably crossed it! It's also not something you want to practice when you're on a cramped train, as you definitely will come across as a pompous—not to mention inconsiderate—prick. Simply walking or standing with a confident posture, crossing your legs and maintaining good eye contact will suffice.

In addition to these core habits, there are several other peripheral habits that you should be aware of. If you remember to use them, great! If not, it won't be the end of the world. In the scenario below, I'm going to show you how and when you should deploy both core and peripheral habits in a typical social situation.

Using Core and Peripheral Body Language Habits

You've just finished a lecture and are meeting a friend at a pub nearby where a social is being held.

Before the event:

You don't always have time to prepare yourself moments before meeting a particular person or group. When you do have a few seconds, however, run a quick check on yourself and fix your body language.

Firstly, check your posture. Personally, I tend to slouch a lot because my head is really heavy and my neck is angled forward. The shape of my spine makes me look a bit like a pigeon if you're looking at me from the side!

Set your posture by pushing your arms back and down. Pretend someone is pulling a string attached to the top of your head.

Check your face and release any tension or wrinkles, particularly around your eyes and forehead.

Start of the event

Small talk is predictable so you can focus on your body language without compromising anything else.

Use 'GESH':

1. **G**enuine Smile: Always smile sincerely and wide enough that your eyes wrinkle. It's easy to tell the difference between a fake smile and a real one. Let the other person know that you're happy to see them even if you've never met them before. This will provide them with an immediate dose of affection and is usually enough to break the ice.

2. **E**ye Contact: Look directly into the other person's pupils, or at their nose, until you feel uncomfortable and then hold that gaze for 1 more second (even if it feels like 5 seconds).

3. **S**tance: Lock them in.

   The next time you're in a public place, take a moment to observe the body language of those around you. Look particularly for groups of 2 and observe how their feet, shoulders and head are positioned relative to each other.

You may find that some conversation partners position their bodies parallel to each other so that their shoulders are aligned and feat pointed towards each other. This is what I call a 'locked in' stance. Each individual is physically showing their interest in the other person. You should always aim to achieve this stance with every interaction you have, especially when it's a 1-on-1. It's often easier if you initiate the stance, so lock yourself in from the moment you meet the individual.

4. **H**and Shake: The next time you're with friends or family ask them about your hand shake. Is it too weak or too strong? Adjust your grip accordingly based on their feedback. If it's too weak then squeeze a little harder than you usually would. Some body language and social coaches emphasise how you should try to close your hand over the other person's because it represents dominance. This is overkill, in my opinion, and it's also nearly impossible if you have small hands. Just make sure you clasp the other person's hand cleanly—don't just grab their fingers.

5. The Hug: This one's more for girls. Make sure your hug is firm too. There is a girl I know who always greets people with a genuine smile and a big firm two-

armed hug. It's so firm that she clasps her own elbows. This is a really good approach which demonstrates warmth and affection.

You will notice that the interaction goes so much easier when you start well. Being admired and respected in any social situation is like flying an airplane. The airport staff and pilots are always involved in the preparation and initial take off. Then autopilot and computers take over once the plane is in the air. In the same way, sorting out your body language beforehand will give you confidence and set you off on the right foot. As others respond positively to your confidence, you'll build momentum. Of course, with any flight, you will experience some turbulence.

During the event

Socialising should feel busy! Once you're in, don't give yourself any time to be self-conscious. If you aren't talking you should be listening; if you aren't listening, you should be talking. If you aren't doing either, you better be dancing or in the toilet, otherwise your mind will start focusing inwards and you don't want to be doing that for long!

You should be so busy that you forget how long you've been in the venue. When someone mentions the time and you're surprised how late it is, that is an indication that you were engaging well with others.

During conversations, don't worry about anything other than your eye contact and space consumption. Have faith that your subconscious is doing a good job on the rest of your body language and make sure you're fully present in the conversations that ensue. In those brief moments where you're not listening or speaking, check your body language.

During large social gatherings, it's also good to be a little tactile. Swathes of research have proven that a simple touch can drastically increase your ability to connect and influence others. Appropriate touching has shown to increase tips for restaurant staff, improve sales conversion rates, persuade individuals to share personal details, solicit help with finding a lost object, and encourage people to sign petitions. These are just a few examples of what the right touch can do. Walking past someone you spoke to earlier? Smile and grab or pat them on the arm. Picture being taken? Get in there, put your arms around everyone and grab their shoulders while you pose. Give hugs and high fives!

End of the event

'What should I do when I feel the conversation is coming to an end?'

Moving from a 'locked in' to a 'locked out' position, is a great way to subtly indicate your intentions to leave. It's best to point one foot away from the other individual and deliver a 'closing line' at the same time. This is something you say to prevent them resenting you for leaving. I usually say, 'Let me grab your number—I'll drop you a message. I want to hear more about xyz' or 'it was great to meet you'.

What Does Bad Body Language Look Like?

1. Nodding Excessively: Moving your head multiple times while listening to someone is a sign of low authority. I did this a lot and still sometimes catch myself doing it on occasion, particularly in noisy bars or clubs. If you want the other person to know you're paying attention, all you need to do is respond in a way that shows them you're listening.

2. Looking at the Floor: There is never a good reason to look at the floor in a social setting. It signals low authority. Would a king or queen ever look down as they enter a room or while talking to others? Of course not. They would keep their chins high and so should you. If you don't cut these habits out now, you may never get rid of them. A few days ago, I met a 52-year-old man who shook my hand and greeted me while looking at the floor!

3. Touching your Neck and Face: Touching the back of your neck is one of the lowest authority signals across the entire animal kingdom.

4. Jerky Movements: Ever met someone who's easily excitable? Usually their body language comes across a little childish. For example, they may make fast jerky movements with their head or hands in the same way a child would if you told them you had a treat for them. Leaders and charismatic individuals are calm and composed at all times.

Body Language Simplified

What you should do:

Core body language habits

1. **Extended eye contact.**

2. **Space consumption with your arms & legs.**

Peripheral body language habits

3. Keep your shoulders back and down.

4. Pretend someone is pulling a piece of string attached to the top your head.

5. Release tensions and wrinkles from your forehead.

6. Use GESH:
    a. Genuine smile

b. Eye contact
c. Stance—lock them in!
d. Hand shake—firm and clean grip.

7. Be tactile!

What you should NOT do:

1. Nod your head excessively.

2. Stare at the floor.

3. Touch your neck and face.

4. Use 'jerky' movements.

Body language isn't complicated and you should ignore any resources or people who suggest otherwise. All you need to do is remember a few core concepts and practice them until they become second nature. Once you're able to effortlessly project affection and authority through your non-verbal communication, you can differentiate yourself from others using your verbal communication.

Chapter 25
Listening. How to Understand them and Ensure they Feel Understood

There are no shortage of books promising to teach you how to speak properly, but very few teaching you how to listen, even though experts agree we should spend more time listening than speaking. The Dalai Lama famously said…

"When you talk, you are only repeating what you already know. But if you listen, you may learn something new."

He makes a good point, but the problem with quotes like this is that they make listening seem like a passive task when it's actually quite the opposite. Good listening requires noticing when others are being vague, encouraging them to express themselves, and seeking clarification to ensure you understand and they feel understood.

Hovering

Very often, during conversations, people hover around a subject instead of tackling it directly. Good listeners can spot this, let the speaker know that they are interested and encourage them to elaborate. For example, let's say your friend is speaking to you about their flatmate:

"Some people can be so inconsiderate sometimes".

I know some people who would immediately respond by talking about themselves:

"Yeah, I know what you mean, just last week...".

A good listener who is social aware should acknowledge when someone is hovering. They should use 'the pause' to see if the other person elaborates on their own.

"The Pause"

Checkout any interview of an influential person (a politician or business leader, for instance) and you'll notice that they pause for at least two seconds before responding. This is an indication of great c-skills. Most people are uncomfortable with any silence when they shouldn't be—gaps during and between turns are normal and there is no need to fill them with 'ums and ahs'.

When someone has spoken, let your facial expressions react first, showing them you have carefully considered what they've said. Only then should you answer. This is the procedure:

1. They finish their sentence.

2. You absorb what has been said for half a breath (roughly 2 seconds).
3. Your face reacts.
4. You respond.

Holding silence may be tricky and awkward at first because you don't know what the other person is thinking, but it's worth the pain.

Practice this regularly and you'll become less sensitive to discomfort. Many of my mentees have mentioned that practicing just this technique alone has improved their interactions.

Encourage

If they don't elaborate after the pause then give them a nudge. I like to use those two magic words:

"Go on..."

Others will appreciate that you're egging them on and giving them room to express themselves. At times, people may not even know what their core point actually is and need a little help. Take it upon yourself to help them find their words.

Clarify

Why did you find that exam hard? Why didn't you put your hand up? Why didn't you enjoy the date?

You don't want to go into interview mode, that would be overkill, your goal is to clarify what they are saying so you can understand them better. Track back if you have to:

"Sorry can we just take a step back…".

"Can we rewind, I just want to understand this a little better…".

Sometimes it's worth clarifying something you may have picked up from reading between the lines. For example, in a conversation I had with a friend at university, we kept going back and forth over what graduate job he wanted to apply for. It was clear he was indecisive and heading towards complete decision paralysis.

"It sounds like you find the sheer number of options overwhelming, and that you fear never making a choice. Am I right?"

He immediately nodded—being a good listener is like being a therapist!

It's difficult to model a conversation, but for a one-on-one interaction it should more or less follow this sequence.

Example 1

Speaker: Hover/vague comment ("Finding a job is not easy")
Listener: Spot and encourage ("I haven't had a real go yet. Why do you say that though?")
Speaker: Reveals core point ("I mean, how am I supposed to know whether I'll enjoy or be good at a job simply by reading two paragraphs on their website?")
Listener (now speaker): Offers their response—a joke, anecdote, fact, opinion ("I don't think we'll ever know for sure unless we try it. The best we can do is speak to people already there and read as much as we can. The rest is a leap of faith!")

Example 2

Speaker: Hover/vague comment ("Finding a job is not easy")
Listener: Spot and encourage ("I haven't had a real go yet. Why do you say that though?")
Speaker: Attempts to reveal core point but doesn't quite get there ("I mean, what to choose?")
Listener: Clarify ("Go on…")
Speaker: Finally reveals core point ("I mean, how am I supposed to know whether I'll enjoy or be good at a job simply by reading two paragraphs on their website?")
Listener: Offers their response—joke, anecdote, fact, opinion etc

One question I get when discussing this topic is: *What if the other person isn't really making any sense, how many times should I try to clarify before changing the subject?*

If depends on who brought up the subject first. If you asked someone about a relationship they're in and they gave a vague response, try to clarify once or twice and if they're still being vague just pivot the conversation elsewhere. On the other hand, if *they* brought the subject up, then it's OK to clarify multiple times.

Empathy

Once, at a birthday party, my friends and I started a conversation with another group. We talked about what everyone was up to in life. Eventually it got around to a girl called Lena:

"I'm in the adult entertainment industry. An adult film actress to be specific".

Everyone went quiet, most looked at the floor or around the room, not knowing how to respond. Jane, one of the girls from my halls of residence, smiled and said:

"Cool—what's your porn name?"

She looked directly into her eyes and I could tell the question came from a genuine place of curiosity. Lena smiled, answered, and the conversation continued as normal.

This sequence of events may seem insignificant but I could see that everyone in the group admired and respected Jane a little more because of her actions.

Firstly, diffusing the tension left by Lena's 'social bombshell' displayed emotional intelligence. Secondly, her nonchalant response projected authority. Finally, Jane put herself in Lena's shoes and understood that most people feel awkward around Lena because of her unusual career choice. By asking a question about her career in the same way she would about anyone else's career, Jane normalised the situation and made Lena feel accepted. This is what empathy looks like.

People are much more likely to open up to you if they think you won't judge them too quickly. By staying open minded and delaying your judgement until you've created a clearer picture, you'll build trust quickly and become a much better listener.

Empathy requires a clear understanding of your own mind and the chaos or weirdness that unfolds inside of it. Most people, if granted a five-minute glimpse into the minds of their friends or family would never view them in the same way again. They would see the crazy day dreams, ridiculous worries, kinky thoughts and dark fantasies, and they would question their sanity. Empathetic people would not be surprised by any of this because they are distinctly aware of the chaos that unfolds in their own heads. Sometimes we focus so much on the faults or quirks of other people that we forget we have an equally faulty mind, filled with same chaos.

So, how do we become less judgemental and more empathetic?

1. Look inwards instead of outwards when you catch yourself judging others.

2. Every person has an interesting story. Walk into all your conversations with the intention to learn more. It's difficult to be curious and judgemental at the same time.

3. Can you relate to someone on their level? Have you shared a similar painful or uncomfortable experience, like a bad breakup or similar career choice? Show people that you understand them because you've experienced what they have.

4. Pause before letting your face react. Furrowed brows will stop people from opening up to you.

Next time someone unusual crosses your path, whether it be a celebrity or a criminal, don't react like everyone else does. Follow these points and you'll be able to empathise with almost anyone. When you've truly mastered this mind-set, if someone reveals that they've murdered someone, you won't flinch and will react with curiosity. That's the way it should be.

Unless, of course, that "someone" is currently buried under their floorboards and they haven't served time or shown remorse. In that case, your expression isn't the issue and you should be running as fast as your legs will take you.

Someone who truly empathises, fully understands the chaos in their own mind so they don't judge as much when they see glimpses of it in others.

Interruption

Good listeners tend not to interrupt and (almost) never let themselves be interrupted. It's easy to become excited about your next thought and to want to get it out of your system before you forget it.

Regardless of how good your point is or if you mean well, the other person will always feel some resentment or frustration after being interrupted. The only time I interrupt is during a group conversation or if someone is yapping on out of nervousness. In these scenarios, apologise for interrupting and steer the conversation into better territory.

If your conversation partner is trying to explain something, interrupting them just because you can't control yourself is a sure-fire way of losing their interest. It shows that you have no genuine interest in them and are only trying to score points. Remember that you're a person of authority; you don't need to prove anything to anyone.

Also, if you think of a good response while your conversation partner is still speaking, don't hold onto it until it's your turn to speak. It will prevent you from listening further, they will suspect your lack of presence and it will be confirmed when you finally get to speak. Learn to let go of those thoughts, keep listening and trust your ability to think of something else.

Just as you shouldn't interrupt others, in most circumstances it's important not to let others interrupt you too. In a group conversation with more than two individuals, one or two interruptions are OK. However, if you constantly let someone stop you, it may seem like you have no back-bone or authority, or that you don't have conviction in what you're saying. If someone keeps butting in, continue speaking as if you haven't even noticed and finish your point. This will maintain your authority and improve the flow of the conversation.

Another situation where you should be open to interruption is during a conversation with someone who has information and power that you don't have. Get curious, listen deeply and ask questions to further your knowledge. Good quality questions will not only give you knowledge-enhancing answers, but also show the other person how present you really are.

High power individuals love talking about themselves. One of my mentees let his interviewer talk for 90% of the interview. He converted it into an offer!

Listening. How to Understand them and Ensure they Feel Understood

- Use 'the pause' before you respond.
- Someone hovering or stuck? Encourage them to elaborate by using these magic words: 'Go on..'
- Clarify to understand and ensure others feel understood.
- Interrupt only when you really have to in a one-on-one conversation.
- You can interrupt more in group conversations.
- As a rule of thumb, never let yourself be interrupted.
- Be un-phased by bad news and unusual people.
- React with curiosity instead of judgement.

Work these habits into your daily interactions with others. Combine effective listening with authoritative and affectionate speaking, and you can handle any social situation!

Chapter 26
How to Mesmerise People with your Words

There is no single way to be, no personality that you have to adopt if you want to be charismatic individual. You can keep most of what makes you unique while still making notable improvements.

As an example, let's look at some people I know:

Ben is inappropriate, tastefully boastful and borderline arrogant, but he can build rapport with anyone in under a minute. Dips is relentlessly nice to everyone and wins the top salesman prize every year at his company. Zainab and Mark use big words that most people don't understand, but they still land date after date. Ashley is borderline offensive and speaks theatrically, but is the most trusted in her circle. All of them are by my definition charismatic and regularly land themselves in the top right-hand side of the judgement chart.

What does this tell us?

While good body language is simple to learn and somewhat formulaic, verbal communication is more of an art form that requires individuality. Every charismatic person has their own unique style and you should too. 90% of the things that come out of your mouth should be unrehearsed. That's why I tread carefully in this chapter; telling you how to think or what to say is counterintuitive and not helpful.

Instead, I'm going to run you through my Do's and Don'ts when it comes to choosing words. Then, using my own examples, along with those from charismatic people in my network, I'll show you how to:

1. Speak in an engaging way.
2. Choose what to say.
3. Tell a captivating story.
4. Use humour effectively.
5. Handle group conversations.

How to Speak so that Others Listen

Your voice is the instrument that delivers content to all those around you. It's important to use it in the best way possible. By projecting your voice properly, you can speak so that others can enjoy listening to you for long periods of time. Your voice can hold someone's attention even when your words aren't that interesting.

Although some people have naturally engaging voices, we can all tune our voices to make them standout and project authority.

So, what should the ideal voice sound like? From listening to hundreds of orators over the years, the best voices have a low baritone sound. Think John Motson, Margret Thatcher and Simon Cowell. We vote for politicians with low-tones. Watch any interviews with these individuals and pay close attention to the low tone of their voices. It's very easy to listen to them for long periods of time. There is a reason why John Motson has been the nation's number one football commentator for over 30 years.

This tone is achieved by projecting sound from the chest or diaphragm. Some naturally speak from this area but most of us speak through the throat or nose, producing a more nasal sound. Have a go now. Try to speak with a nasal voice, then your normal voice and finally go deeper, speaking through your chest. Hear the difference?

You may have noticed that it's difficult to speak from the chest without your lungs being full of air. This is why it's important to speak at a moderate to slow pace. By speaking at a 100mph, you'll need to take shallow breaths to maintain your pace. At this speed, you may initially achieve the right tone, but as you continue it will become pinched. Go slow, breathe deeply and pause often so that your lungs have plenty of air as you speak.

Project your default voice from the chest at slow-moderate pace with a low tone.

Speaking continuously with your 'default voice' will eventually put people to sleep so you'll need play with your sound, especially if you're speaking to a crowd. Have you heard the phrase 'mono-tone'? What others rarely mention is that you don't want a mono-anything: mono-volume, mono-pitch, mono-speed, mono-style.

Vary your voice. Experiment with breathiness and punctuated syllables. Speed up as you build to a climax and then whisper as you deliver it. Embrace silence. There's nothing wrong with keeping others hanging and you don't need to fill it with 'ums' and 'ahs'.

This is what you should avoid:

1. ***Broadcasting:*** Imposing your sound on others around you.

2. ***Intonating the end of your sentences:*** This is when you raise your pitch, making it seem like you're asking a question even when you're making a statement. A lot of people do this when saying their names. When someone asks what my name is, I should say Anshul Raja-(flat) not Anshul Raj-a-a. The latter makes it sound like I'm unsure of my own name and uncertainty is not authoritative.

3. ***Speaking quickly at a high pitch and tone:*** This will give people a headache after a while.

Voices can be projected better by warming them up. Our lips, tongue and vocal chords can become flimsy when we haven't used them much. Have you ever started a conversation after a long period of not saying anything? Sometimes the first word can come out choked or at a much higher tone than anticipated. This can be a little embarrassing. Warming up pumps blood to the body parts that control sound and gives you more control.

Here are some quick ways to warmup:

1. Vocal Chords: Stand up, open your mouth wide, say 'ahh' and bounce on your heels.
2. Lips: Say 'Ba. Ba. Ba' with force. Keep your lips loose but closed and blow air through them making a 'Brrrr' sound.
3. Tongue: Roll your tongue to make the 'Rrrr' sound. Like 'Rrrrrrihana'.

Actors and singers warmup their voices this way before going on stage. I recommend using the above exercises before any high-stakes situation, particularly if you have a lazy tongue and tend to fumble or stutter.

Maintaining a steady, baritone voice with occasional variations, avoiding bad habits and warming up will help you achieve an authoritative sound. This, combined with good body language, will make you standout for the right reasons in any social situation.

The last piece of the puzzle is your content or 'what you choose to say'. It doesn't matter if you sound like Morgan Freeman, if the quality of your content is not great, people won't listen for long.

Verbal Content

Improving the quality of your content is a life-long endeavour. I tread carefully as I write this part of the book because the last thing I want to do is put words in your mouth. Only you can choose what to talk about. However, I can provide guidelines that will help you filter some of your content.

What NOT to do

Gossiping: In our continuous efforts to find common ground with others, we often find ourselves talking negatively about common friends or acquaintances. When someone starts gossiping about someone else, chances are they'll do the same to you when your back is turned. It's a vicious cycle that you're best staying out of!

Judging: Everyone is going through their own personal battles you know nothing about—learn to forgive and not judge. Also, know the difference between judging and being critical:

Judging: 'You are boring'—this is a judgmental attack on someone's personality or character.

Criticism: 'You are being boring'—your opinion on how the other person is behaving in that moment. It might not seem like there is a big difference, but words do matter!

Complaining: TV shows like Karl Pilkington's 'An Idiot Abroad' and 'The Moaning of Life' rack-up millions of views because complaining is our nation's favourite pastime! It's easy to join in the moaning spree around BREXIT or Tuition Fees or the next hot topic, especially when it's difficult to find common ground. Remember, there is a difference between complaining and giving a negative view.

Complaining: 'Our job prospects are going to be rubbish'.

Negative View: 'I think the economy and job market will take a hit'.

Spinning a little negativity with a joke is a good way to pivot the conversation: 'I don't want to be holding 'HIRE ME' signs in Canary Wharf! We need to think outside the box, any ideas?'

Excuses: Don't let others think you're a blamer. Some people never take responsibility and blame others for everything.

Lying: Lies are like social potholes. Every time you tell a fib, you create a hurdle you may trip over in the future. The bigger the lie, the harder you fall; the more lies you tell, the more likely you'll fall. Sometimes even the smallest of lies can snowball into a very damaging situation. One particular story comes to mind:

My friend Raj was visiting from America and was browsing through Tinder late one evening (as you do). He swiped a few hundred girls with no luck, reached his free quota, bought the subscription, and swiped another few hundred until he matched with a girl called Meera. Raj sensed that she wasn't really interested and was only speaking to him because she was bored. She later confirmed that was true!

They messaged for hours and really hit it off. Raj learned that Meera was a highflying oil & gas engineer, University of Cambridge graduate and real estate investor. She openly said that she had been married once before but the relationship ended because her ex-husband lied about having a child.

Messaging turned into phone calls, which turned into an 8 month relationship with marriage on the horizon. Raj even introduced her to his parents. One evening he and I were chatting over the kitchen table when he received a call. It was Meera. He went outside to take it then returned five minutes later looking confused and distressed. Meera had just broken up with him!

She used a recent medical diagnosis as the reason for doing so. Raj was visibly distraught and, after discussing it for hours, we both knew that it wasn't adding up. He called back several times the next day until she picked up and then he asked her to tell him the truth. She burst into tears and replied:

"I'm so sorry but I lied about my career. I'm not an oil and gas engineer from Cambridge. I flunked uni and have been in and out of jobs for a while. Now I'm back at college doing something else".

Raj was shocked! He didn't care about her career or how much money she was making. Why did she lie in the first place? It wouldn't have been a big deal if she came clean early on in the relationship as everyone bends the truth a little on Tinder. It was the fact that she maintained the lie for so many months which made it shocking. Raj had asked her about work on a daily basis and she had replied with comments like "I'm a specialist in reservoir engineering" or "it was really cold on the rig today". Meera even discussed her career with Raj's parents. When Raj asked why she didn't tell him earlier, she replied:

"I met you on Tinder! I thought it was just a fling and never thought it would turn into a proper relationship. You work in America and I never thought we would last this long. You told your parents that I was an engineer! I couldn't find the right time to tell you and the longer it went on, the harder it became to open up. I know this is a long shot, but is there any way you can forgive me?"

Meera became trapped by her first fib. Raj chose to give her another chance but it was pointless. Their trust was badly broken and he began doubting everything she said. They eventually parted ways for good.

It proves that even the smallest of lies can snowball into something uncontrollable. Try to be as honest and authentic as possible. It's so much easier living life without constantly thinking, 'What was it that I told them?'

Exaggeration: Continuously describing every student night as 'awesome' will reduce your authority!

Dogmatism: This is when you phrase your opinions as facts. 'All BREXITers are racists' or 'Remainers don't care about Britain' are dogmatic statements. Any belief or opinion can be dogmatised. We become dogmatic when we lose the ability to admit that what we believe to be true is not the only truth out there. Nothing has an *absolute* quality of greatness or awfulness. Each person feels relative to their own experience. Express your opinions by starting with 'I think..' or 'In my opinion...' or 'I might be wrong but...' to avoid sounding dogmatic.

Boasting: When you express authority through your body language and avoid boasting about yourself, it draws curiosity from others. This is particularly true in low-stake scenarios. People will naturally probe to see what your credentials are and ask questions like: What university do you go to? What course do you study? Have you done any work experience or internships, if so, where? In my opinion, it's best to respond to these questions with brief answers and not to elaborate unless asked to. After answering, ask them the same questions back and look to ask broader questions afterwards. If you use the techniques in this book, others will be more inquisitive about you and your story.

Awesome people don't have to sell themselves. If you're subtle and modest, people will naturally think you're awesome as the conversation develops.

Negativity: In the awkwardness of everyday social interactions it's easy to begin a negative conversation about other people or current events, but do your best to avoid this! Negativity is very draining. If the majority of your conversation was negative, you'll be associated with that negativity. If another person is being negative, there are plenty of ways you can pivot the conversation. Don't take the bait—be a sturdy pillar of positivity that doesn't stir in the face of social awkwardness and temptation.

'Small minds discuss people. Average minds discuss events. Great minds discuss ideas.'

What TO do

Be warm: Jealousy is our lowest-level emotion and causes all sorts of social damage. Wishing people well is the best way to keep this annoying emotion at bay. It's impossible to feel jealous towards others if you're constantly rooting for them to succeed. Congratulate people when they win, encourage them when they lose, and like their Instagram posts!

Compliments are a very good way to show interest in someone else. However, leaving a compliment hanging on its own increases tension. The person you're complimenting starts to think, What does this person want? It's important that you neutralise that tension by moving on quickly, preferably with a joke. This is called the 'push-pull' technique.

Stay honest: People will sometimes try and catch you out with loaded questions. For example:

'Do you still cheat on your boyfriend?'

Response 1: 'No'—Implies you have cheated on him in the past.

Response 2: 'Yes'—Implies you currently cheat on him.

Choosing to answer in the frame that the question is asked leaves you with a lose-lose outcome. Either you have cheated on him in the past or are currently cheating on him. Instead, change the frame of the question and respond by:

Using sarcasm—'Only with his dad ;)'

Breaking the context—'Yes. It used to bother him but now he accepts that Ben and Jerry are staying in my life and there's nothing he can do about it!'

Never feel pressured to answer the question in the frame it was asked. Using humour and sarcasm is the best way to manage loaded questions as refusing to answer can make you appear guilty.

Act with integrity: Ensure your beliefs, words and actions are in synchronicity. Live in accordance with your principles even when it isn't convenient.

Always do what you say you will; talk the talk and walk the walk. Avoid publicly announcing your commitments. Promises and claims are remembered even when you think they aren't. Each failed commitment is a knock to your integrity so avoid making promises unless you're sure you can keep them. If someone tries to get you to commit when you don't have to, stand your ground. On those occasions where you do need to commit, under promise and over deliver!

Always have impeccable integrity and honesty. Every single time you tell a lie, even if it's a little one like 'I'm on my way' when you actually just got out of the shower, or a big one which could come back to haunt you, you're setting yourself up for failure. Even if you don't get caught, you build a reputation within yourself that you are sometimes not to be believed. This affects the conviction with which you speak. You want to be able to look someone in the eye and say, “I believe in everything I say 100%.”

If you do slip up and tell a lie that you can’t undo, never reveal it to anyone. I’ve met individuals who openly boast about being deceptive in sales jobs. I appreciate that sales staff may need to exaggerate or phrase their points in a more persuasive way to close deals, but openly boasting about how you swindled someone to make others laugh is a demonstration of low value. They might laugh at your stories but they’re also thinking that you’re a bad person and making a mental note not to trust what you say.

Be clear & concise: Know your audience and avoid using jargon. We live in a world with growing words ‘Globe-Global-Globalise-Globalisation’ so we sometimes find ourselves using large words we don’t need to. Using language that others understand is more important than using big words to sound intelligent. You project more authority if others can understand what you’re saying the first time you say it.

Donald Trump does this very well. Love or hate him, his communication and persuasive language has been central to his election as US president. Trump uses cognitive fluency bias to his advantage. This is a fancy term used to describe how people are more likely to believe you when using simple language.

Stay structured: Keep your explanations structured.

1. Problem—the National Health Service (NHS) may not exist in 10 years.
2. Solution—to save it, first we need to consider ABC, then we need to consider XYZ.
3. Benefit—doing so will result in...

1. Opportunity—I think we could save the NHS if...
2. Action –first we do ABC, then we do XYZ
3. Benefit – doing so will result in...

1. What?—the NHS is in trouble because...
2. So what (why it's important)?—waiting times are rising and we may not even have the NHS in 10 years...
3. Now what (what are the next steps)?—I think if we do ABC then XYZ, it will result in...

1. Who?—Steven Case is a doctor at my local trust.
2. Why they are important?—he has been very vocal against the changes in the NHS.
3. Now what we are going to do—I'm planning to start a Facebook group to raise awareness for him. Do you want to get involved?

Personal: Many people tend to use distancing language. For example, 'One must consider the ramifications' or 'step 1, step 2, step 3'. People will listen more if you use conversational language. So instead of saying, 'Step 1, step 2, step 3', you could say 'First we need to consider…' , 'Secondly…'

Visual language: What's more memorable? Saying:

'12,000 people die of aids every week'

or

'12,000 people die of aids every week. That's equivalent to an Airbus 747 full of people crashing every day'.

Most people don't like numbers because they can't picture them, and find this type of language easier to remember.

Use these guidelines to help filter your content. None of this information is ground breaking but you'll be surprised at how much verbal garbage people let themselves blurt out. I once asked a mentee to stick to these rules for one full week. The task forced her to listen more carefully to others and come up with better quality content. She later said it had transformed her social life.

Real life social networks aren't much different from online ones in this respect—the stronger your content the more friends you make, followers you attract and likes you receive.

How to Tell a Great Story

We can't talk about storytelling without mentioning comedians. In my opinion, comedians like Michael McIntyre and Russell Brand are the best storytellers out there. One particular American comedian and actor, Jamie Fox, stands head and shoulders above the rest.

Before reading the rest of this section, check out Jamie Fox's interview on the New York radio station Hot97 about filming the opening scene of the new Mike Tyson movie. What you'll see is a master class in storytelling and speaking. Take a look at the comments and you'll see that I'm not the only one who feels this way about him. There is a science to what performers like Jamie do. Here's how they do it:

Firstly, they demand attention and let others know they are about to tell a story. In Jamie's video, he says, 'Let me give you the opening of the movie' and pauses. This prepares everyone for what's to come. It tells others, 'I'm going to talk for a little while so pay attention'. His pause builds anticipation and suspense. This interview was quite a low energy conversation so the hosts kept quiet and let him speak.

In a high-energy conversation where people are speaking, sometimes it's difficult to get a word in. In these scenarios, you may have to be forceful and louder. Raise your voice and say, 'Hold on, listen..'. Say it again if you need to until you have their attention. Regardless of the energy in the conversation, never jump right into a story without having everyone's attention.

Secondly, great storytellers commit fully to their story once they've started. When Jamie took that short pause before beginning the story it felt as though he was getting into character or putting himself in the scene. For the rest of the story he explained all the details as if he was there, even describing the sounds and temperature. He used visual and sensory language to do this. For example, at one point he created a sound effect of a beating heart to describe the heightened emotions in the movie.

Make sure there is congruency between what you are explaining and your body language. If you are explaining an embarrassing situation, pull an embarrassed expression and close your body language. Keep your hands free and let them go where they want as you speak.

Thirdly, they adapt their voices to the events in the story. Watch the video again and notice how Jamie alternates between high and low volume, sped-up and slowed-down. Also, for the majority of the story he speaks through the chest in a slow pace just as I described in the previous chapter.

Lastly, experiment. The stories you hear comedians tell on stage have been refined by repeatedly telling them in day to day low-stakes situations. You should do this too and observe reactions.

Did they enjoy it? Genuine or polite laughs? Did you keep them on edge? Yes. Great, you could probably use that again. Did anyone have trouble understanding a certain part and did you have to repeat yourself? If so, slow down and go into more detail next time. Keep the bits that work and remove the ones that don't.

Many of the largest companies, governments, institutions and religions use stories to communicate ideas. There is a very good reason for this—stories are memorable and often invoke the biggest emotional reactions from us, particularly when we can relate to them. We are more likely to remember a good story than a set of independently listed facts. Also, when you wrap information up as a story it becomes easier to digest, more so than individual statements. Whether they are informative or humorous, stories are essential if you truly want to be charismatic and connect with others.

Humour

You are thirty times more likely to laugh if there are people around you. That is why canned laughter is used in sitcoms like Friends and The Big Bang Theory. Laughing is inherently a social behaviour that we have evolved to help us connect with others. It releases endorphins, a morphine-like compound that creates a sense of euphoria. These dampen the effects of hormones that contribute to social anxiety, mainly adrenaline and cortisol.

There is room for humour even in the most structured or 'serious' of situations, such as a panel interview or negotiation. It's also a great conversational tool that can break down awkwardness and boost the attention span of others. Good, well-timed humour can also help you resolve arguments quicker and disarm those who are frustrated or angry. In fact, humour, when used correctly, can be one of your most powerful assets.

Self-deprecation or Humble Arrogance?

'Shows how much I know'.

When self-deprecating, you are verbally devaluing yourself while simultaneously and indirectly increasing your value. It tells everyone that you're secure and don't take yourself too seriously. Showing a little vulnerability from time to time draws affection and builds trust, but this is only true if you use it sparingly. Unfortunately, many people, particularly British women, self-deprecate far too much out of fear of coming across as arrogant.

In an 18-month study linguistics expert Dr Judith Baxter looked at the speech patterns of men and women at meetings held in seven large companies, including two FTSE 100 firms. An analysis of the 600,000 words used during the meetings found that 80% of the humour used by men was described as 'off-the-cuff witticisms or banter', as reported by the Guardian. About 90% of the responses were positive and resulted in laughter.

However, 70% of the humour used by the women was self-deprecating and 80% of the responses were met with silence. Is it because women aren't funny? Of course not! But there are fewer female comedians than males and it is less culturally acceptable for women to use 'witty banter'. This will hopefully change over time, but if you are a woman there are a few things you can do to create a level footing.

If we take a look at the top female comedians in the world, such as Amy Schumer, they have mastered self-deprecation to a tee. They have done it from a base of self-acceptance and have therefore maintained, if not raised, their social value. So, what can we learn from them?

If you're going to self-deprecate, do it from a place of confidence, rather than using it to gauge the opinion of others or to cement a narrative of worthlessness.

Taboo and Risky Jokes

Unless there is a clear purpose to a conversation, I'm always looking to nudge it into a light hearted slightly inappropriate area. This is because I don't find neutral conversations, such as those based on careers and current events, to be very stimulating, and I think most people agree with me.

Most people stick with conversations about the weather, current events and what they do at university to avoid offending anyone. There is nothing wrong with this, but my approach is different. I'd rather be in that minority of people who walk the line, take social risks and occasionally stumble and embarrass themselves, but are remembered for being original and interesting.

Unfortunately, for every twenty people I meet, I probably end up rubbing one the wrong way! Humour is subjective and that's why it's important to profile your crowd before choosing your joke. A taboo meninist/feminist joke or a safe PG 13 pun? In most cases you'll instinctively know what to pick. When you're not sure, test the waters and keep your eyes peeled for clues.

Do they swear? Do they use slang like 'chill'? Is their top button undone? Are they loud? If the evidence stacks up, a taboo story or joke probably won't offend.

You'll make the wrong read every now and again and it's always awkward when this happens, but as long as you don't make a big deal out of it, no one else will either. If you do something wrong, do it with gusto and state the obvious:

'Oops, borderline—anyway…'

'Wrong crowd—anyway, moving on…'

'I see that was a little taboo…'

I recently met a member of a popular UK boy band at an opening party. The first part of the conversation was very neutral, going back and forth with a few jokes. It was tailing off a little so I made a small inappropriate remark just to test the waters. It was about how musicians take drugs to get their creative juices flowing. The timing was completely off, I forced it, and it was all very uncomfortable. However, I didn't make a big deal out of it and pivoted the conversation. Even though my risk didn't fully pay off, his reaction told me everything I needed to know and the rest of the conversation went much better. If you don't test the boundaries, you'll never know where they are.

Group Conversations

Back in the day I often found myself four minutes deep into a group conversation without a single contribution. As each second passed without me opening my mouth, I would grow more self-conscious about my lack of contribution. Audit trail:

00:00:01 Has anyone noticed?
00:00:02 I should have given my opinion on that earlier thing
00:00:03 Why didn't I speak up when I had the chance?

Eventually I'd snap and force myself to say something. Of course, whatever came out my mouth wouldn't really add much value because I spent more time in my own head than listening to what everyone was saying.

After reading the above, you probably reacted in one of two ways:

1. That is me!
2. What the hell is wrong with you? You need to chill out.

If you are number 2, tell me about it! As for number 1s: To stop this from happening you need to assert yourself early in the conversation.

You can do this in a number of ways, but I personally like to be the first person to break the initial tension in the group. When a conversation with three or more people begins, there is often some slightly awkward small talk. Then, one person in the group takes the initiative to break the tension with a joke, comment, question or some other contribution which moves the conversation on. Be that person!

It's a little uncomfortable to make the first move but the others will appreciate your risk and subconsciously place you at the top of the group. If the risk pays off, you'll find that others in the group will start directing their contributions at you more than the rest. This will give you a big confidence boost.

If the risk doesn't fully pay off, be relentless! If your initial joke didn't come off well or some of your opinions aren't hitting the mark, don't be disheartened. Keep listening and keep contributing until they do.

Secondly, noticeably react to what is being said in the conversation. If someone said a joke you found funny, then laugh—loudly! If someone expressed an opinion you agree with, let them know. Assert yourself in the group. It's OK to be a little more intense and energetic in group situations than in normal one-on-one conversations.

Thirdly, interrupt when you need to but in the correct way. This works for both one-on-one and group conversations. You can do this by using an interjection. For example, if you've been to Mexico before and they mention a trip there, you could follow the conversation with your own personal anecdote or corroborate the speaker's views on Mexico. For example, "Yea, I went to Gran Cenote too, did you dive from the top? Scary stuff' By adding a small but relevant interjection, the speaker can continue and avoid any resentment for the interruption. It also creates a topic you can talk about later.

Another option is to ask a question related to something they mentioned. This works particularly well when you want to pivot the conversation elsewhere. For example, if the conversation about travelling is dragging on a bit and they mention driving across New Zealand, you could then pivot the conversation to cars by asking, "What car?" Interrupting with a question enables the other person to continue contributing but on another topic.

Fourthly, involve other quiet members of the group. You've probably heard this one before, but it's worth emphasising again. Pre-university in my shy phase, I loved those people who opened up the circle and pushed me in. Make eye-contact with and direct conversation towards those who have just joined the conversation or don't seem to be contributing much. They will appreciate the gesture!

Of course, there are quiet people who have no interest in joining the conversation and won't be happy if you keep dragging them into it. The more socially aware you are, the more you'll learn to separate the ones who are painfully shy from the ones who are bored, distant, or otherwise not interested. Pay attention to how they react when others talk. Are they looking interested and smiling here and there, or do they seem vacant? If it's the former, they're probably shy; if it's the latter, they may just be bored and not interested.

How to Mesmerise People with your Words

If you're not sure how you're going to remember all that has been said and use it on dates and at events, don't worry. Most of it is intuitive and will come naturally when you adhere to the basic principles in this book. As for the rest, there are three takeaways that will help you on your way:

1. Project your default voice from the chest at slow-moderate pace and with a low tone.

2. Command the attention of your whole audience before starting a story.

3. Take social risks and recover with 'gusto' when the risk fails.

Chapter 27
Ego Profiling

If I asked you to write a 400-word biography, you would probably write down your name followed by vague statements like:

I care about my family
I'm pretty hard working
I'm ambitious
I have integrity
I'm a good student
I'm healthy
I enjoy playing sport
I'm good with numbers

Your ego is made up from the collective beliefs you have about yourself. Whether these beliefs are true or not doesn't really matter, what matters is that *you* believe them. Many of your day-to-day decisions, from choosing a date to deciding on a career, are governed by this set of beliefs.

Learning to read and interpret the ego of others is an important skill, but understanding your own ego is equally important as it prevents you from being influenced into making wrong decisions.

What Does my Ego Look Like?

Your ego doesn't like being contradicted. If you strongly identify as someone who is fair and honest, it hurts when someone implies that you're greedy. Conversely, it feels good when someone compliments you on how caring you are to your family. Hence the phrase 'stroking your ego'.

We have a number of beliefs about ourselves, but there are a few *core* ones that standout from the rest. Mine all revolve around my ambition: I believe that I'm honest, creative, a good businessman and have a ridiculously good work ethic. These are the first characteristics that come to mind when I describe myself and they are the ones I'm most proud of.

My nearest and dearest, unfortunately, know this! When I get into a disagreement with any of them, they know exactly which buttons to press and how to manipulate me into doing what they want.

For example, if my girlfriend wants me to accompany her to a party that I'm not keen on, she will position it as an 'opportunity to network', naming one or two individuals that I may want to learn from or partner with. Describing the event as 'fun' or telling me it's at a 'cool bar' won't motivate me and she knows that. Over time, as I understood my own ego, these tactics no longer worked as well.

This may sound conniving and sneaky. However, either on a subconscious or conscious level, we all naturally try to influence those around us. It's a psychological game that everyone plays and the stakes can change at any moment. I call it the 'game of influence'.

What Does your Ego Look Like?

To learn more about your ego you should first identify your peripheral beliefs. For example, I have a reasonably good dress sense and overall appearance. If someone were to make a negative reference to my clothes, I'd give zero f****. They could call me ugly and I wouldn't care. It may sting a little initially but I'd get over it in a second and wouldn't dwell on it for long. There are some people out there who identify strongly with having a good appearance and many of them would think about a comment like this for days.

Based on these reactions I know my looks and fashion sense are not core parts of my ego. However, if they made any negative reference to my creativity or work ethic, it would sting more and I would definitely dwell on it. Despite everything I understand about myself, I already know that every negative review I receive for this book will sting badly because it contradicts my core belief that I'm a good creative person who is making a difference to people's lives. Monitoring yourself in this way and detecting pleasure or pain points is good way of identifying the core characteristics of your own ego. Similar concepts can be used to profile others too.

How do we Read Someone Else's Ego?

By observing your interactions with individuals and their interactions with others, you can establish their core beliefs. Did they react badly to a comment made about them on social media? How do they respond to certain criticisms? How do they react to certain compliments? What do they talk about the most—Family, money, girls/guys, success, good grades, charity, politics, sex? A person's ego tends not to change much over time so once you've established their profile, you can use that to your advantage far into the future.

One of my mentors, Mr P, gave me an example of how he used the profile of one of his employees, Sabin, to prevent him from stealing. Sabin was the manager of Mr P's business in the Congo, Africa. He was in charge of collecting precious metals and stones from miners in the surrounding villages.

As you can imagine, integrity and honesty aren't as prevalent in the Congo as they are in the UK. It's like the wild west! It's not that the people are inherently bad, but rather that they are desperate, downtrodden, and often controlled by bloodthirsty gangs and cartels. As a result, there is a lot of lying, stealing and scamming and it's very difficult to trust people—especially in the gold and diamond industry!

Sabin identified as an intelligent person. Mr P first realised this when he thanked and complimented Sabin for solving a small problem for him. He said something along the lines of, "You're quite smart" and Sabin reacted like a toddler. He smiled from ear-to-ear and enthusiastically worked for the remainder of the day. Mr P complimented him for various jobs before, but his reaction to being called 'smart' stood out.

This, among many other similar observations, lead Mr P to believe that 'intelligence' was a core part of his employee's ego. To prevent Sabin from stealing, Mr P associated honesty and loyalty with intelligence. This is one of many WhatsApp messages Mr P sent to Sabin:

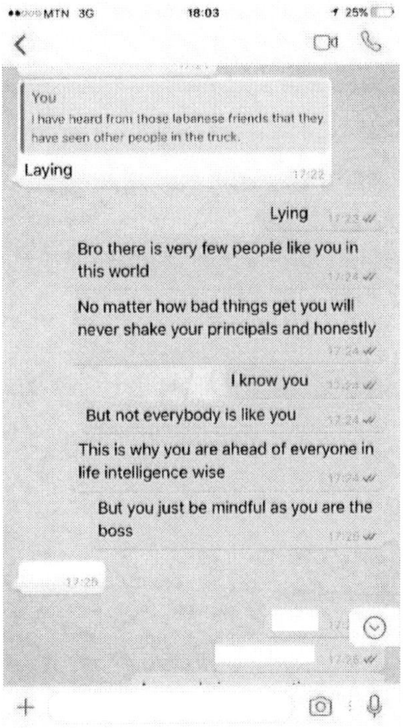

Reading between the lines Mr P is saying:

1. Intelligent people are honest and don't cheat.
2. You are intelligent.

This is an example of *ego-profiling*. A term used to describe when you use the core characteristics of a person's ego to influence their decisions. Stealing, or even thinking about stealing, will become a little more uncomfortable for Sabin. Obviously, this doesn't completely remove the possibility of it happening. If his family are desperate for money and he has no other choice, there's a good chance he'll sneak a few diamonds in his sock. However, *ego-profiling* reduces the chances of it happening and prevents greed being the main driving force.

Sabin ego-profiled Mr P right back! Sabin knew that Mr P identified with having a good reputation and being successful and he used this to increase his salary!

Either on a subconscious or conscious level, we all naturally try to influence those around us. It's a psychological game that everyone plays and the stakes can change at any moment. I call it the 'game of influence'.

Manipulation vs Influence

"Isn't this all just about getting people to do what they don't want to do?"

Ego-profiling is a tool. Just like any tool, how it's used depends on the underlying motivation of the person who wields it. A screwdriver can be used to build your Ikea wardrobe or threaten someone to hand over their wallet. It's your personal responsibility to ensure that your motivations are pure, you maintain integrity and you are always ethical.

This is easier said than done. Sometimes the line between influence and manipulation can be very fine. For example, during a university design project my teammate, Sinji, was getting his calculations wrong. This error was affecting the group's mark, but not our individual grades.

Unfortunately, Sinji's ego identified strongly with being right and meticulous. Whenever anyone implied that he was wrong he would take it personally and dig his heels in. As a result, he shut down all the other team members who tried to reason with him.

In theory, if I got him to do what I wanted, our overall group mark would probably be higher. This would undoubtedly benefit me and the rest of the team. However, regardless of how much each of us chipped in to help him, there was a risk that he wouldn't finish on time and therefore score a lower individual mark. I still felt that even if his individual mark suffered, the average across both group and individual marks would have still left him and all of us better off.

How sure was I of my theory? About 70%. So, with careful wording over a few conversations I used his ego-profile to influence him to do it my way.

Is this influence or manipulation? What if I was 60% sure or thought there was a 50-50 chance or less? If I was 90% sure and turned out to be completely wrong, would I have been a horrible manipulator? You probably guessed by now that there is no right answer when it comes to decisions like this. You can tie yourself into knots thinking about probabilities, ethics and what's right or wrong. There are grey areas everywhere in life and this is my least favourite one. My way of dealing with the ethical part of the equation is by asking myself:

"By ego-profiling this person, is there a strong chance I'll end up hurting them in any way? Am I betraying their trust? Will they be at a disadvantage if I get them to do what I want?"

No = Influence
Yes = Manipulation

How to be a Good Player?

Some people have a knack for this stuff and my girlfriend is one of them. Influencing others comes so naturally to her that when I ask her about it she can't really explain her actions. Mr P, on the other hand, had to develop his skills over time. As with most big paradigm shifts Mr P's started with anguish and pain. He fell victim one too many times at the hand of good players in his personal, academic and professional lives.

"Why do I keep getting run over?"
-Mr P

The mistake most people make at this stage is to ignore or resent the game. People develop this moral righteousness and feel it's below them to partake in such heinous manipulation!

Mr P accepted that others were going to influence and manipulate him regardless. He acknowledged the game exists and then made a commitment to himself to become a better player. All of this started at university.

His approach was to sell. To sell himself, his ideas, his products—everything. His life became one big Dragon's Den and remains that way to this day. In any given year, most of us would have 4 or 5 situations where we need to really influence someone. During the second year of uni, he claims that the majority of his interactions involved some kind of selling. In his words:

"By exposing yourself to so many different types of people, you start building profiles of them. Certain characteristics and egos pop up again and again. Then, as you start speaking to someone new, their comments or behaviour will remind you of someone else you met in the past. You will start saying things like 'that's a Jay' or 'that's a Sarah'."

Influential people have a database of profiles in their head and can recognise new ones easily. That is one of the reasons Mr P is so good at adapting himself to whoever he comes face to face with. Whether it's an attractive girl, a celebrity or a potential billionaire sheik investor he can look past the public façade and see the ego.

"Everyone has pain points and triggers. Most people react when certain buttons are pushed. Anger, Embarrassment, Jealousy. Usually these will become apparent at some point, especially with those you work with or speak to regularly. However, not everyone screams and shouts. Some people are passive aggressive and show their anger by talking behind your back or giving you the cold shoulder."

The same emotion can be projected either assertively or passively. You need to be a social detective. Everyone's going to get their buttons pushed and lose the plot at some point. However, it's not always going to be the same reaction.

"You also can't always play it safe. If something needs to be said or you feel a certain way, you need to say it regardless of the outcome. It will occasionally piss people off or hurt their feelings, but that's the only way you'll learn."

It's important to probe and test people's boundaries. Sometimes that's the only way you can find out where they exist.

Ego Profiling

1. Sell as much as you can

If you have to work part-time in university, pick a customer-centric job, such as an estate agent or salesperson, where you need to influence people on a daily basis.

2. Practice reading people and profiling

Give people 'live reads' where you share your initial thoughts on someone after speaking to them for a few minutes:

'I sense you are a very health conscious, possibly vegetarian or vegan—you probably have MyFitness Pal on your phone. Am I right?'

3. Build your database

Think about your current circle of friends and family. Take a moment to evaluate the core characteristics of their egos and write them down. Compare and contrast. Do any of them share the same characteristics? Can you think of situations in the past which either hurt or stroked their egos? Triggers, pain and pleasure points which prove your evaluation? Taking an almost academic approach to psychology can help you make accurate reads when you are 'out in the field' speaking and influencing others.

4. Know your own ego

Write down the top three characteristics of your own ego. Remember that some people already know these things about you. For the rest of your life, others will come to learn them and may even use them to manipulate you. Knowing your own ego is one thing but detaching yourself from it is another. Some of the mindfulness techniques I show you in the 6-Month Charisma Project can help you separate yourself from your ego and therefore prevent others from playing you like a puppet.

Grujems

Picture this: You're on a date with a very attractive person that your friends have validated. It starts off a little dull. Your jokes aren't really landing and they seem a little preoccupied, probably for reasons unrelated to you. For the first ten minutes, you persevere with little luck. You now have two options:

1. Keep trying to find common ground
2. Go to the toilet and climb out the window

Or there's a third option:

3. Use a Grujem

GRuJeMs. This is a terrible attempt at an acronym for Games, Riddles, Jokes and Magic. Having a few of these up your sleeve can work wonders during stale conversations and raise your social value. Here are a collection of my favourite Grujems:

Chapter 28
Games

People who liven-up dull situations come out on top during almost all types of situations, even in typically 'serious' scenarios with work colleagues.

My mentee, Serena, was given a four-month temporary placement in Dubai to replace someone on maternity leave. The job was in sales and involved entertaining clients, which she had never done before. Two days into the role and with limited knowledge about the products, she was thrown into a meeting with some big Middle Eastern clients at a fancy bar.

Serena and her manager initially struggled to build rapport with the clients because of language and cultural differences. It wasn't an easy sell and the conversation deflated rapidly.

"Do you know how to play fives?"

Interrupting her manager, Serena took a small social risk and asked the clients dressed in traditional emirate white robes if they wanted to play a game. They agreed and it worked!

Both clients found the game hilarious and they loosened up. The conversation that followed became much smoother, with everyone bouncing off one another.

Two days later, Serena received a call from the clients asking to meet and discuss her offer in further detail. Her manager later closed the deal! Serena was offered a full-time position with a pay rise in Dubai after the four months were up!

Keeping a few Grujems up your sleeve can work wonders for you. Games, in particular, are a great way to break down barriers between people. Here are some of my favourites:

Fives

Simple and easy to explain, fives is always a hit. This game is similar to rock paper scissors in the sense that each player is trying to predict everyone else's actions. Here's how you play:

Step 1: Start by multiplying the number of people playing by 5. This is the maximum number. If, for example, you have 6 people playing then the maximum number is 30.

Step 2: All the players make a fist with their right hand and raise it in front of them. Everyone should be able to see each other's fists.

Next, you will count to 3 and everyone in the group (including you) will either keep their fists closed or open them. It's your job to predict what the final score is.

A closed fist represents ZERO

An open hand represents FIVE

For example, let's say there are six players including you. If three players keep their fists closed and the other three open them, the score is 15.

0 + 0 + 0 + 5 + 5 + 5 = 15

Step 3: Count to 3, and on 3 shout out your prediction (e.g. 15!). At this exact moment, everyone in the circle should either open their fist or keep it closed.

Step 4: If your prediction was right, you win! You now step out of the game and become an observer while the remaining players continue.

If your prediction was wrong, you stay in the game and the person to your left becomes the predictor.

The last person left in the game loses. This is traditionally a drinking game so the loser has to drink the entire contents of their cup.

Frog

Frog is great for large groups. I organised this game with over 20 people during fresher's week. There are 3 phrases you need to know for this game:

- 1 Frog
- Jumped in a pond
- Plop

Let's say you're in a group of 4 people. As the first player, you shout out "1 FROG TO MY LEFT". The person to your left (player 2) then shouts out "JUMPED IN A POND". The third "PLOP". The fourth "2 FROGS".

Now it's your turn again and you continue: "2 FROGS".

Player 2: "JUMPED IN A POND".

Player 3: "JUMPED IN A POND"

Player 4: "PLOP"

You: "PLOP"

Player 2: 3 FROGS

Player 3: 3 FROGS

Player 4: 3 FROGS

You: JUMPED IN A POND

Player 2: JUMPED IN A POND

Player 3: JUMPED IN A POND

Player 4: PLOP

You: PLOP

Player 2: PLOP

Player 3: 4 FROGS

The person who loses count or hesitates has to drink. Sounds a bit lame, but after about 5 FROGS this game becomes quite challenging and fun. It's hilarious when people mess up!

Going to the Moon

Each player has to choose an item to take to the moon. But, you can't just take any item because there is a rule that determines what you can and cannot take. The objective is to guess the rule as quickly as possible. You, as the organiser, create that rule and share it discretely with one other person in the group. The best rule to start with is, 'You can only take an item that starts with the first letter of your name'. So as Anshul, I could take an Apple, Anaconda, Alien, etc., but cannot take a Space Ship, Golf Club, Rocket, etc.,

After both of you clearly understand the rule, each person in the group takes turns to say, 'I'm going to the moon and I'm taking a....' and name their item. It's not as obvious as it sounds and there will be some players who get it right away and some who scratch their head for the whole game!

Heads Up

Inspired by Pictionary and Charades, this is an awesome game app made by Warner Bros. It even records gameplay on your phone so you can play it back to yourself. It has been a hit every time I've used it and is a great Grujem!

Never Have I Ever (NHIE)

In this game, each person in the group takes turns saying the phrase, 'Never have I ever…' followed by an action. For example, 'Never have I ever…read Harry Potter'. If you have read any of the Harry Potter books, you take a sip of your drink. If you haven't, you don't have to do anything.

This is a personal favourite of mine because it breaks through ice like a sledgehammer. 'Never have I ever read Harry Potter' can very quickly turn into 'Never have I ever had a tattoo in an awkward place'! In the spirit of the game, players start revealing details of their lives that would normally take many hours of trust building. Everyone's walls come down and it becomes much easier to build connections.

Games like NHIE also help you profile others quickly. Did anyone object to playing the game, react negatively to a borderline comment, or stay quiet throughout? If so, you'll know exactly where their boundaries are and discover who you'll get along with.

Chapter 29
Riddles

Always have a few brain teasers, riddles and puzzles up your sleeve. Keep a collection of short or medium length riddles that you can rattle off to a group in a noisy bar. Longer riddles are best used in quiet surroundings with fewer people. Here are my top picks:

Top Riddles – Short

1. What stays in the corner but travels all around the world?

2. What comes once in a minute, twice in a moment but not once in a thousand years?

3. What is the coolest letter in the alphabet?

4. What two words, when combined, contain the most letters?

1. A stamp
2. The letter M
3. B (always surrounded by AC)
4. Post box

Top Riddles - Medium

1. People come to visit me but usually don't stay for very long. I can be clean but am more often than not very dirty. People usually reveal to me a part of themselves that they rarely show others. What am I?

2. This thing all things devours: Birds, beasts, trees, flowers; Gnaws iron, bites steel; Grinds hard stones to meal; Slays king, ruins towns, and beats high mountain down.

3. Imagine today is the end of the world. There are zombies, snakes and lava closing in on you from all directions. You have with you only a dirty sock, a plastic straw and a ripped piece of paper. How can you possibly get out of a situation like this?

Answers

1. A toilet
2. Time
3. Stop imagining :)

Top Riddles - Long

1. A man lives in the penthouse of an apartment building. Every morning he takes the elevator down to the lobby and leaves the building. Upon his return, however, he can only travel halfway up in the elevator and has to take stairs for the rest of the way—unless it's raining. What is the explanation for this?

2. Three people check into a hotel room. The receptionist says the bill is £30, so each guest pays £10. Later the clerk realises the bill should only be £25. To rectify this, he gives the bellboy £5 to return to the guests. On the way to the room, the bellboy realises that he cannot divide the money equally. As the guests didn't know the total of the revised bill, the bellboy decides to just give each guest £1 and keep £2 as a tip for himself. Each guest got £1 back, so now each guest only paid £9, bringing the total paid to £27. The bellboy has £2. And £27 + £2 = £29 so, if the guests originally handed over £30, what happened to the remaining £1?

Answers

1. He is short and can't reach the top button for the high floors so he takes the stairs. However, when it's raining, he carries an umbrella which he uses to press the top button in the lift.

2. There is no missing pound. The men spent £27. Of which £25 went on the room and £2 went to the bell boy. You cannot add the £2 the bellboy has to the £27 the men spent as this £2 actually comes out of the £27 the men spent. Put another way, consider how the £30 breaks down: £25 – room. £3 (3x £1) back to the men. £2 Bellboy.

Chapter 30
Jokes

I've had a lot of direct and indirect experience with stand-up comedy and comedy in general, from improvised comedy training to interviewing stand-up comedians and experimenting on and off stage. There are a few things I have learnt, one of which is that taboo, racist, sexist, feminist, meninist—basically all '–ist' jokes—always seem to be hits (with the right crowd). These are my preference. However, taboo jokes aren't always right for every person or situation so it's important to have a few PG-13 jokes in your memory bank.

Of all the genres I've come across, anti-humour or anti-jokes are my favourite. These are indirectly funny and make use of big anti-climaxes. It's not everyone's cup of tea but they almost always get a laugh. Delivery is very important with anti-jokes. The punchline needs to be delivered in a way that makes it clear that the anti-climax, in fact, *is* the punchline. Here are two of my favourites:

Millennial Moth

A millennial moth went to visit a paediatrician. He sat down on the patient's chair and the doctor said, 'How can I help?' The moth, with tears in his eyes, said, "Listen doctor, everything is going wrong in my life."

--

I've spent the last decade on my smart phone and on social media so now I'm socially anxious and awkward all the time. The other day someone said hello to me and I responded by saying, 'I'm fine thanks, how are you?'

My job is horrible. I'm not fulfilled by what I do. I'm not making any impact. Every time I ask my boss how I'm doing she scowls at me and says that I shouldn't ask her 10x times a day. When I was younger, I assumed I would be a millionaire and buy a big house. My parents said I could change the world but no matter how many invoices I file, I get no closer to solving world poverty.

My parents don't understand me—they just tell me to get on with it.

My friends think I'm selfish and self-centred.

I'm no longer the moth that I used to be.

--

"I'm not in a good place doctor."

The doctor said, 'It sounds like you need to see a psychiatrist, why did you come to see me?'

The moth shrugged and said, 'Because the light was on'.

Man with the Big Orange Head

A man walks into a bar and sees a guy with a big orange head just sitting there, sipping and swirling his drink. The man asks the bartender, "Say, what's up with the guy with the big orange head?" And the bartender says, "It's an interesting story. Buy him a drink and maybe he'll tell you."

The man walks over, introduces himself and offers to buy a round. The guy with the big orange head says, "Yeah, I'll bet you want to know the story, huh?" To which the man replies, "Sure, if you don't mind." The man with the big orange head sighs and says, "You know, I've gone over it in my mind a million times.

Basically, it's like this; I was walking along the beach one day, when I stubbed my toe on something. I looked down, and there was an antique brass lamp. I picked it up and dusted it off a little, when all of a sudden this enormous genie pops out, yelling, 'You have released me from my ten-thousand-year imprisonment. I am now in your debt and I will grant you three wishes as a token of my gratitude.'"

The man at the bar is agape. The guy with the big orange head continues: "So I said, 'Wow, okay. Well, my first wish is to be fantastically wealthy.' The genie says, 'Your wish is granted.' And all of a sudden I have rings on my fingers, and a crown on my head. My wallet is full of money, a dozen credit cards and the deed to a mansion—I mean, I was loaded! So I said, 'Amazing! Okay, for my next wish, I want to be married to the most beautiful woman in the world.' The genie says, 'Your wish is granted.' The ocean parts, and out walks this gorgeous woman in this beautiful dress, and she links arms with me and we fall in love and the genie marries us right there. It was incredible. The genie booms, "You have one wish remaining." The man with the big orange head pauses and sips his beer. He says, "Now, you know, this may be where I went wrong. I wished for a big orange head."

Anti-humour

Didn't get it? With the big orange head, you assume he's going to screw up his last wish somehow, since his head is orange, but the joke is that he didn't screw it up. That's exactly what he asked for! With anti-humour the entire time you're reading or listening, you're expecting a climatic ending to the joke when in reality there is no joke. That's why, with the correct delivery, these jokes are hilarious! It's a classic bait and switch. Screwing with people's expectations is a great source of humour.

Another reason I like anti-humour is because you can adapt them to any stereotype. For example, you can turn the Millennial Moth into the Vegan Moth and go into a creative monologue about vegan problems:

'No one listens to my detailed statistics about animal cruelty or vaping or Cross Fit'

'I have to send the food back ten times in a restaurant'

'I'm tired of hearing "plants have feelings too"'

You can also shorten these jokes:

The millennial moth went to visit a paediatrician. He sat down on the patient's chair and the doctor said, 'How can I help?' The moth, with tears in his eyes, said, "Listen doctor everything is going wrong in my life. My girlfriend hates me, my job is rubbish and my friends think I'm self-centred. I'm not in a good place doctor.

The paediatrician said, 'It sounds like you need to see a psychiatrist, why did you come to see me?'

The moth replied, "The light was on"

Here are some more short ones…

Anti-humour—Short

What's worse than stepping on dog poo?... Death

What's green and has wheels? Grass. I lied about the wheels.

Why was six afraid of seven? It wasn't. Numbers are not sentient and thus incapable of feeling fear.

What did the lawyer say to the other lawyer? We are both lawyers.

A duck walked into a bar…and was quickly escorted out as no ducks were allowed in the bar.

Just as you would with your stories, test out all your jokes in low-stakes situations before telling them to your boss or on a date. Use feedback to adapt the jokes and make them your own.

Chapter 31
Magic

In the Canadian TV show 'Keys to the VIP', male candidates compete to seduce women in bars and public places. As shallow as this show sounds, it was actually a great social experiment. One of the contestants on the show happened to be a magician. His verbal and body language skills were OK. He was an average looking guy (search for the episode and you can judge for yourself).

I thought he would come across like a street entertainer who was trying too hard. I mean, who brings props and cards into a bar? But he surprised me and the judges on the panel. While making his way through the venue approaching various women, he spoke little and performed various cheesy tricks like turning a napkin into a floating rose. It was shockingly effective!

Most of the men loved him and the women adored him. Nobody cared that he had props. He was so much more interesting and unique than everyone else. Even if there were a few haters, they were the ones with their backs to the wall looking at women as they walked by. He was the one connecting with new people and enjoying himself. He won the episode and was voted the best contestant out of the whole series.

You would think that carrying props around with you everywhere is a little desperate. However, people just want to enjoy themselves and connect. Helping them achieve that will only increase your social value.

Also, magic is universally loved. Its appeal transcends different cultures and languages. If you can look past some of the negative stigmas associated with magic and learn a trick or two, you'll have tool that can help you influence and connect with anyone.

What Magic Should I Learn?

The internet is filled with tutorials of magic tricks, but not all of them are appropriate or effective for social situations. I have listed a few below that are perfect as they are easy to remember and perform and they don't come across as contrived or painstakingly rehearsed.

1. **Mentalism**—think Darren Brown! Mentalists create the impression that they can read minds, predict the future and achieve other psychological feats. For example, asking someone to pick a number between 1 and 10 then 'reading their mind'.

2. **Street Magic**—think David Blane or Dynamo! Street magicians often use props, such as fake thumbs and playing cards. Many tricks use sleight of hand and distractions to deceive and amaze the audience.

Mentalism

Given that we're using magic to raise social value, mentalism is the obvious choice. We don't need to carry around any props and can perform tricks to anyone at any time.

'Illuminati' is my favourite mentalism trick.

Illuminati

This trick is also known as 'triangle in a circle' and works best in one-on-one situations. First you stand or sit directly in front of your target person, take a deep breath and say:

"I'd like you to imagine a screen between you and I."

As you speak, press your index fingers and thumbs together as if you're holding two bags of crisps and then draw a rectangular screen with both your hands. Say:

"On that screen, imagine a shape like a square but not a square."

As you say this line, pretend you're holding the base of a triangle with your index fingers and thumbs. Make it look natural. It doesn't need to be obvious.

"Lock it in."

"Got it?"

Wait for their response and say:

"Project another shape and put that around the shape you already have."

Draw a partial circle with both your index fingers as you say "the shape". It shouldn't be obvious and can be a quick gesture.

"Got it?"

"Excellent."

Now you have to pretend that something serious is happening. Strain your face, wrinkle your brow and ask them to:

"Project this right into my eyes and to the back of my head. Please concentrate."

Hold eye contact for a couple seconds and then release the tension in your face, saying:

"It's a triangle inside a circle!"

If you follow the steps above and move through them fairly quickly, nine times out of ten you will 'guess' correctly.

Street Magic

As effective mentalism can be, the reactions I've received from performing street magic tricks have been much stronger. One person almost fell off their chair in shock!

As I mentioned before, using props won't lower your social value but it's a lot of hassle. Some props are awkward to carry around all the time and you'll probably end up losing them. Ideally, you want to shock and surprise using the least amount of apparatus possible.

Coin magic is the best choice if you have the time to learn and regularly practice it. Asking your target to give you a coin or taking one out of your pocket feels spontaneous and unrehearsed. Coin magic is unfortunately difficult to learn and requires continuous practice otherwise you'll get rusty and fumble the tricks. It's not really practical from a charisma perspective and that's why I prefer using playing cards. My favourite trick is the 3-card diamond monte.

3-Card Diamond Monte

Have you ever seen those street hustlers sitting in popular tourist locations shifting around 3 bent cards on a table? Usually they make bets with passers by and hustle them out of money. The 3-card diamond monte is a variation of that trick!

As the name suggests, this trick uses three playing cards which are specially made and can be ordered online for a few quid. You will need to use the 'double lift' to perform it properly. This is a technique which fools people into thinking you've picked one card from a pile when you've actually picked up two. Good double lifts take some practice to learn. I used to keep a set of cards in the bathroom and practice a few lifts when I had some time to kill. Over time it became second nature.

There are some great tutorials for these tricks online and it's easier to learn them by watching an expert do it. I was taught by an expert magician and then tuned it up using YouTube videos. I suggest you do the same. Invest in a set of these cards, learn the trick and always keep them in your wallet or hand bag.

If you want to research and learn more tricks, go for it, but just remember to keep it simple. It's easy to get carried away when learning magic because there are so many awesome tricks.

You're not trying to be a magician here, but just someone who knows a little magic.

Online Charisma

Chapter 32
Social Media Influencer

At the time of writing, 5 billion of us own smartphones. Facebook, YouTube, Instagram and Twitter are visited by four billion of us every month. Why? Firstly, social media is fun! Jokes, arguments, memes—the list goes on. Also, people like being social and part of a community whether it's in real life or online. These platforms appeal to one of our strongest evolutionary desires: to be accepted and validated by others. Whether it's being followed or retweeted, we receive a hit of dopamine each time.

Beyond connecting with others and being entertained, can we use these platforms to our advantage? And if so, how? Can social media hurt our charisma? Let's find out:

Hurtful or Helpful?

Social media can be addictive and it can skew our perceptions of the world, making us paranoid, insecure, and depleting our self-worth. Studies looking at the effects of social media on mental health have found some worrying results. One particular survey done by a leading psychologist found that a large number of people experience 'feelings of inadequacy and anxiety' as a direct result of using social platforms.

One of my mentees, Sara, was spending up to 5 hours a day across Facebook messenger, WhatsApp, SnapChat and Instagram. She openly admitted that it made her unproductive and unhappy. Like most, she looked for social validation by checking the number of viewers on SnapChat or likes on Instagram. Everyone does this and it is normal to want others to approve or like you. In fact, a study in the United States found that people checked their phone every 12 minutes, or 80 times a day, and there have been similar results in smaller, UK studies. But Sara was going above and beyond what could be considered “normal”. She was logging-in an unhealthy number of times a day and couldn’t stop comparing herself to celebrities and Instagram influencers.

She acknowledged there was an issue and that she needed to stop. She tried turning her notifications off, using control apps and even getting her flatmates to hide the phone. None of it worked. Eventually, she went cold turkey for several months and it solved the problem!

The whole saga felt like a drug detox, with similar highs and lows, yet we were dealing with an ostensibly harmless activity that everyone has access to. It’s supposed to be harmless, but for some people it's anything but, and if you fall into this category it’s probably worth doing what Sara did. If social media is negatively impacting your self-esteem, then it’s not going to help your charisma and it’s probably best that you skip this chapter.

This is as far as I'll go discussing the negative effects of social media. When first writing this part of the book, I wrote a whole section on all the arguments for and against using social media. Then a YouTube influencer and friend of mine sent me this quote.

'Dear pessimist, optimist and realist. While you guys were busy arguing about the glass of water, I drank it.'

Sincerely,
The Opportunist'

Everyone is arguing about whether it's good or bad. In my opinion, energy and time is better spent discussing if and how we can use these platforms to our advantage.

Can Social Media Help our Charisma?

If your goal is to strengthen your existing relationships, grow your influence with others and create new connections, then publishing content online can help.

As we've discussed throughout this book, charismatic people project authority and affection while being present, and it's possible to project these traits online, to an extent. The problem is, broadcasting our personality in this way is a one-sided interaction: when you upload a story to Instagram or Snap Chat, everyone can see your body language and hear what you say, but you can't see their reaction or response. Trust is built via two-way interactions—being in the presence of one another, moving past the initial awkwardness, reacting to words, observing body language. These are the building blocks of trust and it's hard to achieve this through one-sided online broadcasting.

What about affection and authority? Can someone come to like and respect you by consuming your content, even though they haven't met you before? Absolutely! Look at the movie and TV industry. Actors, musicians, politicians and sports stars—viewers build affection for these people through technology all the time.

People can Build Affection Towards you Through their Phones and Computers.

The annals of history are littered with people who got their big breaks and earned their place in the public spotlight because of their talents, from great singers and entertainers, to authors and entrepreneurs. But these are different times and you don't necessarily need to be talented to earn your fifteen minutes of fame.

Kim Kardashian was the most googled person in 2014 and has been in the top 3 ever since. She doesn't sing, act, innovate or have any talent in the traditional sense. However, she knows how to project charisma and brand herself online. The Kardashians have used mainstream media and social media to build their following, but there are countless others who have done it solely through posting content online. Myself included.

Having amassed a following of over 40,000 people across several social platforms, it has had a noticeable impact on my social life. Old acquaintances who didn't give me the time of day before I had a following became unusually nice. During high school, there was one individual who wasn't particularly friendly with me. He was a real King Joffrey, the kind of person who thought they were above everyone else, and I wasn't the only one who had this opinion of him. At a recent reunion I tried my best to converse with him and to be nice, but he was abrupt and rude—clearly the years hadn't mellowed him or made him any less obnoxious. The very next week I bumped into him at a birthday party and he was unusually friendly. Then he dropped me an Emoji-laden message with even more pleasantries. I didn't think anything of it until one of my other friends mentioned how he spoke to King Joffrey about How to ACE. It all made sense after that!

On another occasion, I was with a prospective client who was a little reluctant to do business with me. While waiting in line to order coffee, the girl standing next to us recognised me and asked:

"Hey, are you Anshul Raja?"

She then explained how she follows me on Facebook and saw my TedX talk on YouTube. The three of us chatted until her coffee came and before leaving, she said:

"I hope you do more talks like that. It really inspired me to do better in my exams. Thank you!"

Just as my head started deflating, she turned around and asked for a selfie! I'm no celebrity, but for that moment I felt like one and my prospective client did too. That incident boosted my social value and permanently changed our relationship. I went from being someone he had to fit in for half an hour to someone he respected and eventually did business with. We closed a lucrative deal and I strongly believe it wouldn't have happened without that selfie!

That student found me because of my TEDx talk which was content I created in my spare time. She approached me because that content added value to her in some way. The TED organisers only asked me to do the talk because they were impressed by my following. Over time, the benefits of investing time into producing online content were becoming more apparent and the disadvantages everyone warned me about never appeared. When I meet new people these days, they very often mention my social following but either don't know about or put much importance on my books or other 'real' achievements!

You don't even need a very big following to experience this charisma boost. A friend of mine went travelling across South America for several months and documented her travels. She posted one picture and several stories a day on Instagram. Her following grew from a few hundred friends and family to 3000. This is by no means a large following, but she came back a new person with a bunch of new friends. Everyone back home treated her differently. The first time I saw her, she worked the room like I had never seen before. Was it the experience of travelling that changed her or the extra followers that came with it? Probably a bit of both.

Online vs Offline Charisma

In some ways, using online platforms to project your personality and charisma can be more effective than doing so in real life. You have more time to think about what to say or write and get second opinions. Not happy with what you published? Edit it and try again. Most platforms provide immediate feedback and data too—followers, likes, shares, views, comments. All of these are luxuries we don't have in real life!

You can also reach out and connect with a lot more people than you would ever be able to in real life. Even if you joined a bunch of different societies and went to every social event, you'd only be able to connect with a few hundred people a year, but online the possibilities are endless.

Depending on how often you publish, the frequency at which your audience see you and consume your content can be really high. Without social media, that person who you spoke to for five minutes during fresher's week would have forgotten who you are and vice versa. But you added them on Instagram, where you publish stories 3 times a day and post great content every few days. It doesn't matter what that content is. You could be sharing your opinions, thoughts, acting out short comedy sketches, singing, playing sports, or gaming. Your personality and charisma will be on display and they will be seeing it several times a week. When they wake up, go to the toilet, scroll through their phone on the train: you'll be there. With respect to charisma and social status, this is revolutionary and is something the previous generation weren't able to take advantage of.

As you have probably gathered by now, because of the reasons outlined above, along with the impact it has had on my life and others I've met, I do recommend having some form of presence online. There is something about putting yourself out there and letting everyone know who you are that people find appealing. If you can look past all the negativity and naysayers, there is a real opportunity here to raise your social value. All you need is a personal branding strategy!

Chapter 33
Personal Online Branding Strategy

Most social media users are there for recreational purposes and don't have an objective. They want to be entertained, to see what their friends and family are up to. They want to **consume content**. If you are serious about building your personal online brand, you will need to **produce content**. What type of content? The options are limitless! If you've had an idea for a blog or YouTube channel, that's a good place to start. However, if you don't have a clue, the next section will point you in the right direction.

Focused Content

What do you do when you aren't working? What content do you consume in your spare time? What are your future career aspirations? Take a few minutes to answers these questions and write them down. Here are some typical answers:

"Mainly socialising. Going out with friends and watching rugby. I would like to go into Management Consulting then maybe start a business someday".
-Stephan

"I love reading. Fiction books mostly. I read over 20 books a year. I really don't have a clue what I want to do! Something in accountancy or business related because that's what I'm doing at uni".
-Kiran

"I'm a bit obsessed with Trance and Deep House. I watch/listen to loads of it on YouTube and follow top DJs on Twitter and Instagram. Future career aspirations? Probably finance or join my dad's business".
-Craig

"I love cats! We have 3 back home and they all have their own twitter accounts! Surprise, surprise—I want to be a vet".
-Nat

While Stephan and Kiran needed a moment to think about their answer, Craig and Nat answered the question almost immediately. His eyes opened up as he spoke. Music was his 'thing' and he's had an interest in that genre for a number of years. It was clear that he had a strong and **focused interest**. If you too have a focused interest, producing content on and around that topic can change your life.

Craig started with a blog and a few social pages which he updated once a week. He eventually started producing his own music and a podcast. This was all during university! Doing all this 'put him on the map'. It gave him a social edge that stayed with him throughout uni and beyond. It even made him a little money, which brings me to my next point.

If you have a focused interest which can be monetised now or in the future, creating content around it should be a no-brainer. Not only would you get the social boost that Craig experienced, but you may also get an income source and a way to differentiate yourself in the graduate job race.

Nat was quite a shy person in high school and was reluctant to put herself out there. Before starting university, she thought that people would think she's weird for loving cats. After all, our feline friends are often synonymous with lonely ladies living in the countryside. However, after a little encouragement, she started publishing various forms of content online all around the topic of caring for cats.

Initially, these were just blog posts, but this changed as she realised that people were very interested in her content. Nat moved from written content to video content and turned the camera on herself. Her popularity skyrocketed and so did her confidence.

At uni, even though she didn't boast or talk about her online platform, people organically found out and it wasn't long before various opportunities started landing on her lap. She spoke at university society events and created written content for small media websites. In her second year at university, she turned it into a business by selling digital and physical products to cat owners.

Unable to secure a place in Vet Medicine during 6th form, in her final year at uni, she reapplied to her first-choice university armed with her online platform and was accepted! Did her platform really help get her into Veterinary medicine? This was her answer:

"There is no doubt that my online platform did boost my CV and personal statement. It impressed them for sure! However, I feel the underlying confidence and charisma that I gained by working on this 'venture' is the real win here. You wouldn't believe how quiet I was back in the day. Many friends and family have noticed a big change in me since 6th form. I mean... everyone changes at university. Whether the change is good or bad depends on the choices you make. From a social/confidence perspective, creating an online personal brand helped me more than any university course could ever have done and it was the best choice I ever made".

Many of the success stories you hear happen when multiple interests line up in the same direction. Creating an online brand improved Nat's social value, income and future career prospects. If your interests line up with your future ambitions in this way, it's worth investing a significant amount of time or even money into building a personal online brand. You owe it to yourself!

One point you should remember, if you currently create focused content or plan on doing so, is to make sure there is a piece of you in everything you publish. Your name or brand name should be easily seen if you are blogging. Don't be afraid to record videos of yourself or post pictures. This isn't a school or university thesis so it's OK to be personal. For example, let's say you're producing content on travel and want to create a podcast on travel tips for Barcelona. Rattling off the pros and cons of visiting Las Ramblas or Camp Nou will do very little for your personal brand. You should speak on the podcast in your own voice, give your opinion and share one or more personal experiences. People are attracted to other people not to facts and figures.

In How to Land Your Dream Graduate Job, I get into the nuts and bolts of focused content creation, from video editing to social media management. I'll walk you through how I used focused content creation to separate myself from the herd, land internship/graduate positions at top firms and build a successful business.

Broad or Personal Content

What if you don't have any focused core interests like Craig and Nat? In my experience, most people don't or are yet to find something they are obsessively interested in. This isn't a problem and you can still produce content:

1. On various parts of your life.

and/or

2. About a broad range of topics.

Chances are, you probably do this already. Do you tweet, post pictures on Instagram or publish stories on SnapChat? If so, you're already producing content about your life and building an online brand. Anything you publish into the public domain is content that is giving an insight into your personality. What you choose to post determines the level of affection and authority others see in you.

What Should you Post?

Whether you are a *focused creator* who invests a lot of time into publishing content or a *casual* one who likes to upload a Instagram story every once in awhile, treat your social media accounts as if they are mainstream media platforms. Every time you post a picture, pretend that it is going to be on the front cover of a magazine for thousands of people to see. This mental exercise will protect your personal brand.

Let's say the Beckhams had a picture of their oldest son, Brooklyn, taking part in charity run and want to share it to a mainstream media platform. Whether it be a published platform like *Hello Magazine* or a broadcasted one like BBC1, there would be a system of checks and balances used before the picture was released. Why? Because, although Brooklyn is an individual, he has a personal brand which has value. Those invested in him want to ensure that value grows over time.

You and I may not have a brand quite like the Beckhams, but we still have one and it still has value. This is why you should have your own set of checks and balances. One way to do this is to separate yourself from your personal brand. When I'm talking to a friend in person my name is Anshul, but if I'm posting anything online I am Anshul Raja Ltd. Doing this mental exercise, helps me look at what I post objectively and it's a reminder that my content is going out into the public domain.

Let's take a look at the three types of content you can publish online and how each affects your charisma.

Words

Whether it be 280 characters on Twitter or a comment on Instagram, words matter. Now that you're approaching your twenties, people tend to judge you on your grammar and spelling. Clean and easy to understand writing will show that you are a good communicator. Make sure you don't lose touch with the basics!

After writing a tweet or a caption on Instagram, pause and take an objective look at what you've written. Is it gossip, judgemental, a complaint, excuse, lie, exaggeration, dogmatic or boastful? If so, have another go at writing it or consider posting about something else.

Have you ever noticed how people put 'All opinions are my own' in their Twitter profiles? Often this is because they don't want their views to be confused with that of the organisation they work for. It's also meant to let people know they aren't dogmatic. Putting IMHO (In my honest opinion) or IMO (In my opinion) before giving your opinion shows people that you understand that what you believe to be true is not the only truth out there. These small considerations matter!

When I notice someone with good social etiquette, it shows that they understand people and have high emotional intelligence. It immediately raises their social value. Give people a reason to like and want to interact with you.

As a rule of thumb, try to be more positive than negative with the content you publish. I know a lot of people bang on about being positive all the time. However, year on year, I keep seeing others fall into these negative spirals that cause them to puke negativity all over their social media pages.

Those who are negative in person tend to be even more negative online because they are behind their phone or PC. On Instagram, the hashtag FML (F my life) has been used 5.6m times while hashtag TGIM (thank god it's Monday) 365,000 times. Positive thinking and its benefits have been explained to us for years yet the majority of us still don't do it.

How you react to others online also has an effect on your social value. Most platforms enable us to easily react to other people's posts. We can like, comment or share on everything. Liking posts which are derogatory or of low social value won't help your online charisma.

Let's say someone has uploaded a post you fundamentally agree with but they've done it in a very dogmatic and offensive way. By liking it, you may come across as dogmatic too. By association, even the people you follow can have an effect on your online personal brand.

Think about all the celebs who have gotten into trouble just for liking a post, from football players getting fined for liking negative posts about their managers, to actors and musicians getting bad press for liking derogatory, racist or homophobic posts. A like is a meaningless, throwaway gesture for the average user, but for anyone with any social standing or any degree of celebrity, it's an endorsement, and one that could hurt their reputation and career. Be wary!

Have you ever been a victim of cyber bullying, a troll or any unwarranted insults online? Did you react with anger and some insults of your own? The majority of people do. People tend to get into arguments online because it's easier to be brave when you aren't looking someone in the eye. When someone attacks me online, I take it as an opportunity to display emotional intelligence and authority. I apologise if my content has offended or bothered someone and ignore blatant trolls.

This may seem like I'm being 'weak' or not defending myself but it has the complete opposite effect. People always gravitate towards those who are emotionally stable and unfazed when under attack. Letting mild negativity or criticism bounce off you shows everyone that you know how to pick your battles and are rock solid. Keep an eye on the bigger picture, control your emotions and let negative comments go in one ear and out the other. You'll always come out on top, especially in the eyes of those trying to inflict abuse.

Intolerable negativity is a different story. This is when someone is being prejudiced or dogmatic towards you. Usually this comes in the form of racism, sexism, ageism and all the other '-isms'. In this scenario, I point out what they are doing without attacking their character. You can do this by criticising their actions. For example, "That is a racist comment", as opposed to, "You are racist".

Lastly, use Emojis! So much information is lost when communicating through written words online. No one can see your facial expressions, body language or hear the tone in your voice. No exclamation mark or round yellow face with its mouth open will ever have the same effect as you opening your eyes wide and saying something with conviction in person. However, they are better than nothing!

I use the smile Emoji the most for the same reason I smile a lot in person. It conveys affection and lets people know I'm coming from a friendly place. It can also prevent disputes and negative feelings caused by miscommunication. How would you feel if your other half WhatsApped you and said:

We need to have a chat

versus:

We need to have a chat 😀

The first line without the Emoji provokes a response of tension and worry, while the second doesn't. Use Emojis!

Pictures

Many of the principles that apply to coming across well in real life social scenarios also apply online. Most of all displaying authority and affection. For example, if you are posting a picture on Instagram, does your body language appear dominant? Take a look at these two cringe worthy pictures of me out with friends.

40 Likes

40 Likes

From everything you've learnt about body language in this book, if you could only pick one, which of these pictures would you choose to post?

If we're talking about authority, even though I look like a bit of a plonker, the first picture wins as I'm pulling the strongest of all power-poses. However, authority is all I project in this picture and as I mentioned before, too much authority can make you appear arrogant and unapproachable. Even though my friends and family know I'm not like that at all, the HR manager at the firm I want to work for or a new friend I'm going to meet next week doesn't. For this reason, I'd probably keep this offline.

However, the second picture ticks both the affection and authority boxes. My pose isn't as dominant as the first picture but I am still taking up space with my right arm and projecting a confident posture. The most important difference with this picture compared to the first one is that I'm smiling and doing so with a friend. This is where the affection comes in. The first picture is aesthetically great and Insta-worthy—I'm dressed better and much cooler. Unfortunately, my inner PR manager won't give it the go ahead!

Videos

TV shows like Big Brother, a game show where participants were filmed 24 hours a day 7 days a week in a house, were the early signs that people enjoyed watching others in a real and unedited way. After this, reality and semi-reality TV shows started appearing all over the place. In the UK we had Geordie Shore, I'm A Celebrity… Get Me Out of Here, The Only Way is Essex, Love Island and many more. This was all in mainstream media.

Social media was the next evolution. It confirmed our desires to see each other's lives in this candid, unedited way. The trend continues as big social platforms have recently invested heavily into Live Streaming in an attempt to make video content even more authentic.

Of all forms of content, video has grown the most over the last 10 years and continues to grow year on year. People are much more inclined to click "play" than read a blog or listen to a podcast. It's for this reason, particularly if you are a *focused content creator*, that you should create engaging videos. What makes a video engaging?

As an avid marketer, I can rattle off several ways you can keep viewers watching such as:

1. Quick changing frames.

2. Clarity and picture quality.

3. Audio quality.

4. Subtitles, if your viewers can't listen to you.

5. Good lighting.

I can go on for ages, but the truth is that most engaging videos contain one common denominator and that is people. People like watching other people. They like seeing their faces, hearing about their triumphs, opinions and concerns. Taking a picture or video of a sunset on its own will never be as engaging as a picture of you in front of the sunset. The picture of you and the sunset will never be as engaging as a video of you looking into the camera and describing how you feel about the sunset.

Whether it's an Instagram story or an upload to your YouTube channel, take lots of videos and ensure your face is in the majority of them. Most people feel more comfortable filming other people or events than turning the camera on themselves. I wouldn't blame you if your immediate thought might be that you don't know what to say in front of the camera or that no one cares what you have to say. They do! Your perspective on the world is unique because it's coming from you and there is no one else in the world like you. Even if you fumble, mumble, stutter or a bunch of garbage comes out of your mouth, it doesn't matter. It's not improvised comedy. You can always delete it and have another go.

Before hitting "record", try to warmup your voice before speaking, using the exercises I described in chapter 26. Speak through the chest and pay attention to your pacing.

When you play it back to yourself before posting, look for the bad habits. Are you nodding excessively? Intonating when you shouldn't? Are there tension wrinkles on your forehead? Not varying your pitch, speed and tone? Have another go. Aside from broadcasting your authority and affection to all your followers, continuously seeing your facial expressions and hearing your speech will help you improve over time.

Another good habit is to keep your eyes locked on the camera lens. Most modern-day cameras, even the ones on smartphones, are very powerful and can pickup pupil movements pretty easily. Staring right at the centre of the black dot is how you keep eye contact with the hundreds or thousands of your viewers.

When Should you Post?

Frequently! There is a sweet spot which is just short of being annoying but enough to create the mere-exposure effect. This is when people tend to like those they are familiar with. In one example of this phenomenon, psychologists at the University of Pittsburgh had four women pose as students in a university psychology class. Each woman showed up in class a different number of times. When experimenters showed male students pictures of the four women, the men gravitated to those women they'd seen more often in class—even though they hadn't interacted with any of them!

From my experience, publishing content to your audience once a day is enough to create this effect. Vary your content between videos, audio, pictures and writing. This will prevent you from becoming annoying and will keep people interested. People might not admit it to your face but they will come to enjoy waking up in the morning and seeing what you have to say!

Putting it all Together

Social media and any online media is only damaging if you let it control you. However, if you can turn the tables and use it as a tool rather than just to pass time, there are big rewards. I used the phrase ‘content creation’ quite a lot and I know this can make it sound quite boring. However, all you're really doing is sharing a part of your world with everyone else. You’ll be surprised how many people are actually interested in you and what you have to say. It might seem like a chore in the beginning, but as people start treating you differently, creating more content will feel effortless and fun. At times, even therapeutic!

Focused, broad or personal? Written, images, audio or video? I hope that I’ve convinced you to have a go and that I’ve provided enough direction to start. Make sure you stay in control and stop yourself from obsessing over likes, shares and followers. Publish information that represents you. Be someone with opinions and beliefs. Engage and respond to others who comment. Be a positive human being. Keep everything legit as your employers will be checking you out.

Charisma Project

From dealing with internal distractions to projecting charisma through social media, we've covered a lot! Now we need to bring it all together and use these techniques in day to day life. When I first started taking my c-skills seriously, every few weeks I'd assign myself a technique or task to focus on. I'd say, "Right, for these two weeks I'm going to practice extended eye contact", and then move on to something else. After a few months, these techniques became second nature and I still apply and benefit from them every day. I've organised all the methods described in the book into a 6-month 12-step Charisma Project.

Each step will take anywhere between a few hours and 2 weeks to complete. Given the sheer number of different concepts and techniques described throughout the book, I'll be summarising these into one line affirmations and acronyms that you should memorise.

Some of the tasks I'll ask you to complete will be uncomfortable and unorthodox. You'll be doing a lot of acting and approaching strangers! All my mentees and clients have enrolled in the 12-Step Charisma Project and many have had incredible life-changing results. In some cases, it has transformed shy and introverted kids into confident young adults who are powerful influencers. Before starting the project, there are a few 'back office' tasks you should complete first.

1. Social Media Spring Clean

Go through any old content you have in the public domain and remove posts that don't fit your personal brand. If you aren't happy deleting old pictures or posts, learn how the privacy settings work on the platforms you use to ensure your content is only seen by people you approve.

Whether you're vetting old or creating new content, use the checklist below to help you decide.

Online Content Checklist

This checklist is designed to be your personal PR guide. Do you want to upload or share a piece of written content, picture or video? Use the scoring systems to decide what to choose.

Want to upload a video or image of yourself?

Are you smiling? If so, 5 points. If not, 0.
Are you with other people? If so, 5 points. If not, 0.

On a scale of 1 to 5:

How genuine is your smile?
Hint: Genuine smile = Your eyes squinting slightly with wrinkles around them and teeth showing.

How much space are you taking up?
Hint: Look at your arms and legs.

How good is your posture?
Hint: Are your ears in line with your shoulders? Looking up or down?

What is the quality of the picture?
0 for poor pixilated or dark and 5 for clear and high definition.

The maximum number of points you can achieve is 30. Ensure any video or photo content you upload has a score of 20 or above.

Want to upload a piece of written content or a video or podcast where you're speaking?

Are you speaking from the chest for more than 70% of the time? If so, 5 points. If not, 0.

Have you varied your pitch, tone, volume and speed at least twice? If so, 5 points. If not, 0.

Are you intonating the end of your sentences when you don't need to? If so, 0. If not, 5.

Are you lying or exaggerating? If yes, 0. If no, 5.

Are you bragging or boasting? If yes, 0. If no, 5.

Are you being dogmatic? If yes, 0. If no, 5.

How well are you communicating?
Hint: Are you hopping all over the place in a way that's difficult to follow (0) or is it clear and structured? (5)

The maximum number of points you can achieve is 35. Ensure your video, audio or written content has a score of 25 or above.

2 – www.firstnamelastname.com

Buy a domain address which contains your full name. For example, if your name is John Smith, buy the domain name www.johnsmith.com or www.johnsmith.co.uk

You can purchase domain addresses from a number of different vendors for affordable annual fees. GoDaddy.com is the vendor I currently use. If you have a very common name and the address isn't available, try www.firstmiddlelastname.com or www.firstname-lastname.com.

Why? Over the next few decades, many people from employers to potential girlfriends/boyfriends will check you out online. You want to make sure the first result they see is a website owned and maintained by you. Creating a website with your name in the URL is the best way to achieve this. Of course, you will also need to populate that site with basic content about yourself.

Thanks to cloud platforms like SquareSpace, building a website has never been easier! You don't need to know how to code HTML or PHP. These platforms enable you to drag and drop content like a PowerPoint presentation. Pick a website builder and start creating content!

3. Success Compilation

Studies done by Oliver Schultheiss showed that we can boost our testosterone levels by watching movies or other video content. Creating your own Success Compilation video can help increase confidence and reduce anxiety. I've already shown you how to do this and discussed how important it is, but here is a quick recap:

1. Accumulate old pictures and videos of proud moments. These should be clips of:
    a. Yourself: Look for proud moments where you displayed powerful body language and

confidence. These could be anything from winning a sports competition in high school to being offered a place at university. Video content which shows you experiencing a proud moment is the most powerful content to use. For example, a video of you going to collect your GCSE results or degree.

   b. People you Admire: These could be historic political figures, celebrities or your mentor.

   c. Friends & Family: Include a few clips of your favourites and those who you want to make proud.

2. Take all the content and stick them into video editing software like 'Windows Movie Maker' or 'iMovies'.
   a. If you don't have time to do it yourself, send the content to a freelancer on Fiverr.com or PeoplePerHour.com and get them to do it. This shouldn't cost you more than £30.

3. Add powerful and inspiring music

   a. Start with a Hans Zimmer type movie soundtrack, preferably from a memorable scene filled with power and inspiration. Gladiator? Lord of the Rings? Hunger Games? You choose!

   b. You can also record and add a message to yourself or have someone you admire record one for you.

4. Compile the video and keep a copy on your phone.

5. Start filming! We capture almost everything on our phones these days, so just shift the focus to proud moments and don't be afraid to make it all about you. When important coursework marks are coming out, keep your phone ready to capture the moment. Get your friends & family involved and try to record genuine emotionally powerful reactions.

   a. Be sure to add clips. My goal is to have an hour-long compilation I can watch when I'm lying prone in a nursing home with tubes up my nose!

Before walking into any high-stakes situation watch this video! It will give you an immediate testosterone and confidence boost.

The Charisma Project

Now that you've cleaned your online content, bought your personal domain name and are armed with a confidence-boosting Success Compilation we can start the 6-Month Charisma Project!

For the project to work, you will need to meet three times as many people over the next 6 months as you normally do. This is crucial for two reasons: Firstly, you will be practicing various techniques over this period and need plenty of people to practice them on. Secondly, increasing your interactions will naturally reduce any social anxiety you have. As we discussed before, anxiety is often half the battle.

I will go as far as to say that even if you were to dismiss all the advice I've outlined in the book and simply maximise the number of people you interact with on a weekly basis, your c-skills will significantly improve! This first step is the most important and I truly hope you follow through. Here's what you should do:

Each day for the next 7 days count how many people you speak with in person or over the phone. Take an average and multiply that by 3. This is the total number of people you need to interact with per week for the remainder of the c-skills project. Keep a tally on your phone to track your interactions.

How do you find people?

Not all of us are social butterflies who can send a mass WhatsApp message and arrange a 200-people strong house party. However, to meet your 3X quota, becoming 'the organiser or host' is a great way to come into contact with more people. Be proactive with your friends, make the effort to arrange meet-ups and encourage friends of friends to join. Use social media. I've had some mentees hit their quota by starting social groups for new freshers and organising meet-ups in various parts of the country.

If all this sounds daunting or time consuming, you can achieve your quota in other ways too. For example, I made a commitment to always say hello to anyone I bumped into from the past. Being socially lazy, I would usually hide or look at my phone if I spotted an old primary school friend on the train or a work acquaintance in a coffee shop. Doing the exact opposite helped me reach my quota each week, particularly at uni.

If you are currently at uni, meeting people becomes much easier as you can always rely on society and career events. Taking on responsibility at a society event is a sure-fire way of regularly meeting more people. Just make sure it is a well-established and large society. The Katie Hopkins Appreciation Society started last year by two final year foreign students isn't going to yield much! I'm a big fan of graduate and internship events too and these are all over the place. You can even attend these if you haven't started uni yet.

Getting a customer-centric part-time job is also a good option. A great, albeit slightly challenging job is where you stand on the street stopping pedestrians and getting them to signup for memberships. It's difficult, but you can hit your quota with just a couple hours of work a day.

Let's face it, people are everywhere. You are only a phone call or instant message away from meeting someone. It's simply a matter of making the effort. Whether you're currently at university or not, get out there and start hitting your quota!

Step 1 - Measure Your C-Skills (Day 1 to 14)

In Chapter 9, I mentioned how the education system does a great job of assessing your i-skills but does little for your c-skills. This is why it's important to objectively assess your charisma sooner rather than later, using:

1. Myers Briggs personality test.
2. Low-stakes career interviews.
3. High-stakes career interviews and assessment centres.
4. Feedback forms.

Myers Briggs

It's very difficult to benchmark our personalities because we're all individuals. Your experiences and genetics have shaped you into the person you are today. However, neuroscientists and psychologists have produced tests to help us understand our personalities better.

Myers Briggs is the best one we've come across and it has been used by hundreds of Fortune 500 companies. The creators Isabel Myers, and her mother, Katherine Briggs identified 16 personality types based on psychological preferences. It uses four measurements:

1. Extrovert and introvert.
2. Sensing or intuition.
3. Thinking and feeling.

4. Judging and perceiving.

In the test, you will be given statements and asked to choose an answer between 1 and 5:

'You prefer to act immediately rather than speculate about various options'.

'You often contemplate the complexity of life'.

'When with a group of people, you enjoy being directly involved and being at the centre of attention'.

Your answers will define which of the 16 personality types you most closely resemble and most online tests should produce a scale like below.

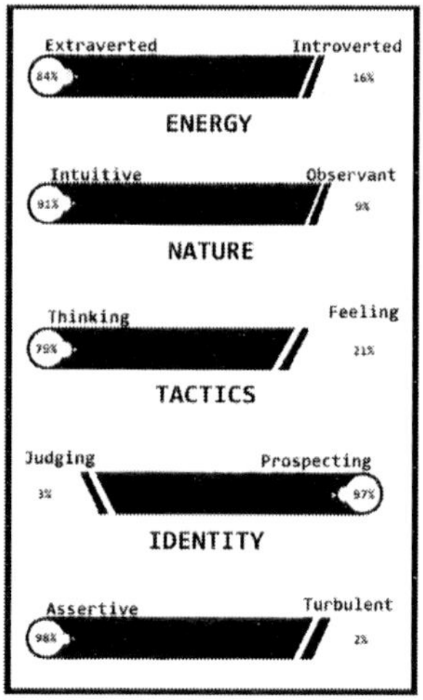

We are interested in the first scale. From testing clients and students, those who are charismatic social influencers tend to be 40% extroverted or higher. One of the most charismatic people I know has a score of 55%, so a high extrovert score does not necessarily mean great c-skills. It's merely one of many indicators you can use to measure your improvement. My personal score at university was 44% Extrovert and 56% Introvert. Now it's closer to 50-50.

Download 'Personality Test LAB' and 'MB Personality Type' on your phone and complete the questionnaires. Be honest with your answers! I also recommend taking one or two more desktop Myers Briggs type tests on www.16personalities.com and www.truity.com. Take an average of your extrovert/introvert scores across all these tests and e-mail it to yourself for future reference.

Low Stakes Career Interviews and Assessment Centres

Over the next two weeks, organise at least one competency based interview with a careers advisor. Most university career centres offer this service for free to all students. In competency based interviews, interviewers ask questions like:

1. Tell me about yourself.
2. What are your strengths and weaknesses?
3. How good are your leadership skills? Give me an example.
4. Can you work in a team? Give me an example.

Here comes the important part—don't prepare for the interview! For the purpose of this exercise, the interview questions are irrelevant and you can blag the answers if you wish. When I did this my response to, 'Give me an example of your leadership skills?' was a story about how I lead the winning team on my scout summer camp aged 14. It was the only example I could remember! If you don't know the answer to a question just be honest about it and try to answer the next one. The objective is to be yourself. That's it!

The interviewer will probably give you feedback on the quality of your answers from a careers perspective. However, we want to find out what the interviewer truly thinks of you as a person. When they go home to speak about their day with their other half and say, "I interviewed this person today. They were…", what words follow? Arrogant? Timid? Unconfident? Interesting? Funny? We want them to push past all the professionalism and BS to reveal their true feelings about you. This is how I did it:

After they give you feedback, go see them in person and handover your own feedback form asking the following 4 questions:

Me-Feedback 1

On a scale of 1 to 10 how much do you like me?

On a scale of 1 to 10 how much do you respect me?

On a scale of 1 to 10 how much do you trust me?

If you were to summarise me in one word what would it be?

If you were to talk about me to your husband, wife, girlfriend, boyfriend, Mum, Dad or sibling—what would you say about me?

Feel free to be brutally honest. I'm a big boy/girl and can handle it! ☺

Let them read the questions for a moment and don't let them answer while you are in the room with them, otherwise the answers will be biased. Look them in the eye and say something like:

"I know the questions may seem a bit odd, but I really want to understand the first impressions I give to people who don't know me very well. If you answer the questions honestly, it will help me understand this and boost my chances of performing well in an interview situation. I'd really appreciate your help!"

When you like and respect someone, it's difficult to pick out the reasons why. It's a feeling based on a number of factors, from body language to personal similarities. This is why we want the questions to be broad as they'll be more blunt and truthful. We want to find out how much affection and authority we project.

Some people hold back because they don't want to hurt people's feelings, so you have to give them a free pass and let them know it's OK to be blunt. Show them how desperate you are for honesty and the reasons why.

High-Stakes Career Interviews and Assessment Centres

As I mentioned in Chapter 9, a high-stakes interview at a top company will give you the best indication of your c-skills. Assessment centres where you have to do group exercises in front of interviewers are even better. Many of these companies invest millions into their human resource departments and train interviewers to separate the weak from the strong. Quite often, as an undergraduate or graduate, they will assess you as a person in addition to your qualifications.

This is why you should first decide what you want to do and then apply to as many internship and graduate programs as possible, particularly in your first two years at uni. Check out the third book in this series, How to Land Your Dream Graduate Job, if you need help in this area.

After each interview, always ask for feedback and don't settle for a generic answer like, 'We felt you didn't provide enough evidence that you are a team player'. Always push and get to their root feelings about you. There have been occasions where I levelled with my interviewer on the phone and said 'come on. What's the real reason you didn't go for me?'. I always had to push 2-3 times before they came out with the truth either because they felt sorry for me or just wanted to get off the phone! It was painful hearing someone criticise my personality, but it did wonders for my charisma.

Feedback Form

Think about your nearest and dearest, the close friends and family that you completely trust. Write their names down and give each of them the following feedback form:

Me-Feedback 2

Dear nearest and dearest,

I have embarked on a 6-month self-development journey to improve my social intelligence and awareness. From making long lasting friendships to persuading interviewers to hire me, this program is going to help me succeed in many different aspects of my life. BUT—I need your help to make it happen!

The reason you have this piece of paper is because you are one of my nearest and dearest who I trust immensely. You are one of a handful of people who know me better than anyone else. It is for this reason, for the purpose of this journey, you are my biggest asset! This request might seem a little out of the box, but I would really appreciate if you could anonymously fill in the form below.

Please be as brutal as you want and don't hold back from telling me the absolute truth (I'm a big boy/girl and can handle it ☺). Honesty is what I really want because that is going to help me improve.

After you are done, I'd appreciate if you could print it out and send it to me.

Yours truly,

Me-Feedback 2

On a scale of 1 to 10, How good are my overall social skills?

Where on this scale do you think I sit?

Shy--Charismatic

When I speak, on a scale of 1 to 10 do I sound quiet or loud? (very quiet being 1 and very loud being 10)

What are some of the positive things people tend to say about me when I leave the room?

What are some of the negative things people tend to say about me when I leave the room (don't worry I can handle it ☺)?

Do I remind you of a celebrity or TV/Movie character? If so which one? (based on personality, not looks)

Again, sometimes it's difficult for close friends and family to give you the honest truth as they don't want to hurt your feelings. By reassuring them that you can handle it and keeping it completely anonymous, they will feel comfortable with being open.

Negative criticism will sting a little but don't take it personally. Try to appreciate it and feel grateful for the honesty. No one on this planet is perfect, we all have our weaknesses. It may not feel like it at first, but honest feedback is one of the biggest gifts anyone can give you.

Despite our request for honesty, they will sugar-coat their feedback. The positives are great, but what we really want to focus on are the negatives and particularly the negatives that appear more than once.

Measure your C-Skills

Measuring your charisma is much more difficult than measuring your ability to write essays or solve problems. Combining Myers Briggs with qualitative feedback is a good way to discover how others perceive you.

The feedback from your interviewers will be the impression you make with someone completely new, while comments from friends and family will reveal 'home truths'. Combining both sets of results will let you know where you stand and make

it easier for you to improve. Even the smallest revelations can motivate you to make lifelong changes.

During high school and uni, four independent people said that I reminded them of Jimmy from the movie American Pie. Jimmy is a very likeable character. However, by the end of the movie if someone asked what you thought of him, all you would have to say is, 'He seems really nice'. Jimmy is a classic example of a character that doesn't project enough authority.

This was one data point, among others, that suggested I sat to the left of this scale:

Affection---Authority

Of course, I already had an idea of the kind of personality I have but sometimes you need someone to confirm it to truly believe and to do something about it.

I thought I was a great hard-working student until I got slapped in the face with D's and U's at A-level. I couldn't run away from those grades, blame the grade boundaries or my teachers. The truth was on a piece of paper glaring back at me. It was only at that point did my beliefs change and journey to improvement begin. Feedback from interviewers, friends and family provided me with the equivalent slap in the face. Only this time it shed light on my c-skills rather than my i-skills.

Among other feedback, the Jimmy comments stuck in my head and pushed me to change. To this day I repeat the following words before walking into any social situation:

'You're not Jimmy'

Thankfully, since final year uni, no one has ever made a connection to Jimmy or any other 'low authority' personality. If anything, thankfully, they associate me with people I admire and want to remind them of.

Step 2: Presence (Day 15 to 30)

For the next two weeks, make a proactive effort to be curious while speaking to people. Use the affirmation ***'every person is an opportunity'*** to stop you from feeling socially lazy and to encourage proactive listening.

Mindfulness

If you've never meditated before, I recommend starting with 'guided meditation' using an app like 'Insight Timer' or 'Headspace'. This is when someone walks you through the technique. Listen to the recordings on the app just before you go to sleep or immediately after waking up. You can pick any guided meditation track and follow the instructions. My personal favourite coach is Sam Harris.

After you become comfortable with the technique, start meditating in silence without using any app or guidance. This is much more difficult because you don't have anyone's voice or music to focus on. However, doing a minimum of 10 minutes of silent meditation every day will get you the best results.

From training with free divers on the Gili Islands, Indonesia, to Buddhist monks on Mount Koyasan, Japan, these are my top tips:

1. Always begin meditating with a tension check. Starting with your forehead and finishing at your toes, release

any muscle tension. You'll be surprised how many muscles are contracted without you noticing, especially the forehead and jaw.

2. Breath with your belly. As you inhale, your torso and stomach should be bloated to the point it looks like you're pregnant.

3. Follow your breath closely from your mouth all the way to your lungs and then back out again.

4. Stop at the first thought. This was the top tip given to me by a Buddhist monk in Japan. He said:

"Let's say you start meditating on an empty stomach. Suddenly a stray thought about Ramen (Japanese noodles) finds its way into your consciousness. This is the first thought. You can either:

1. Catch the thought and focus back on your breath.

Or

2. Think about your favourite Ramen restaurant that you want to go to for lunch.

Number 1 is good technique and 2 is bad technique."

Regular meditation combined with an open minded and curious attitude towards others will help you remain present during conversations. However, even the most charismatic people can doze off sometimes. After all, we're only human and not everyone is as engaging as Russell Brand or Jamie Foxx. The eyelash snap is a useful trick we can keep up our sleeves to help us mid-conversation.

Eyelash Snap

This is a great technique that I use all the time. Whenever you catch yourself distracted from a conversation, do the following:

1. Nod your head slightly.
2. Focus on one eyelash closely.
3. Wait for it to blink.
4. Snap back into the conversation.

People tend to fix their heads when they lose concentration during a conversation. Nodding *slightly* will stop your conversation partner from detecting your lack of focus. Some also tend to look down or away when distracted. By focusing on an eyelash, you always maintain eye contact and give yourself a little time to get back into the conversation without letting the other person know that you dozed off.

Presence: Day 15 to 30

Over the next 2 weeks focus completely on being present in all areas of your life. Whether it be listening to a mono-toned lecturer or a conversation with your closest friend, your goal is to focus and absorb everything they say.

1. Continuously think or say out loud the affirmation:

"Every person is an opportunity"

2. Practice the eyelash snap at least three times a day.

3. Download a meditation app either Insight Timer or Headspace.

    a. From days 1 to 7, practice guided meditation for a minimum of ten minutes a day either before bed or as soon as you wake up.
    b. From days 8 to 14, practice silent meditation for a minimum of ten minutes.

Step 3: Authority and Affection (Day 31 to 45)

Projecting both a high level of authority and affection through your body language and spoken word is the key to being charismatic. As I mentioned in Chapter 12, if you project more authority than affection, people will feel you are unapproachable and arrogant. Too much affection and little authority, people won't respect you. Balancing both is difficult because there is such a fine line between being truly liked and disliked, but there is an even finer line between being respected and pitied. Taking on an alter ego and experimenting with various personalities will help you test the limits and find that balance.

Over the next 2 weeks, you're going to conduct a social experiment that will push you right out of your comfort zone. Meet your alter egos:

High Authority—Low Affection

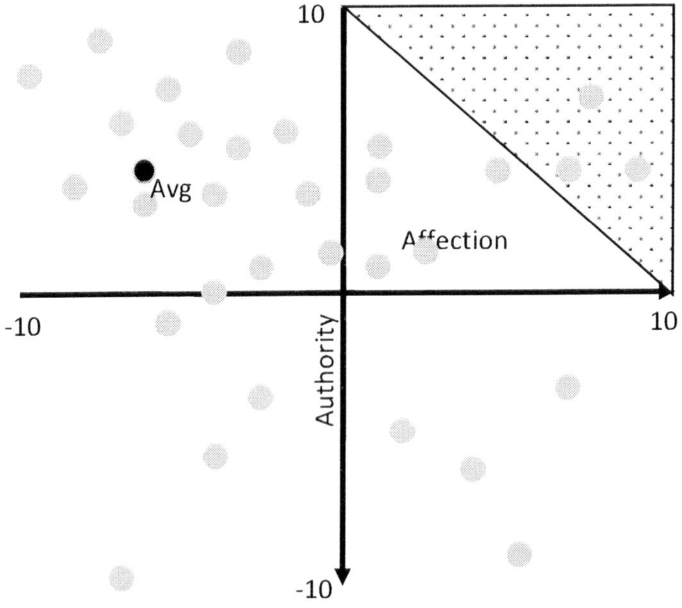

Tara

- Her friends and family would describe her as 'ultra sassy' and 'a bit of a b**** sometimes'.
- Movie characters or celebrities she is often compared to: Cersei Lannister (Game of Thrones), Olivia Pope (Scandal), Karren Brady (The Apprentice UK), Miley Cyrus.

Steve

- His friends would describe him as 'uber-confident', 'arrogant' and 'a bit of a prick sometimes'.
- Movie characters or celebrities, he is often compared to: Donald Trump, King Joffrey (Game of Thrones), Alan Sugar (The Apprentice).

Tara and Steve:

- never let anyone cut them off when speaking.
- rarely ask questions about anyone else's lives.
- dominate conversations.
- never speak quietly.
- jump into the middle of a group when a picture is being taken.
- speak from the chest with a low baritone sound.

Low Authority—High Affection

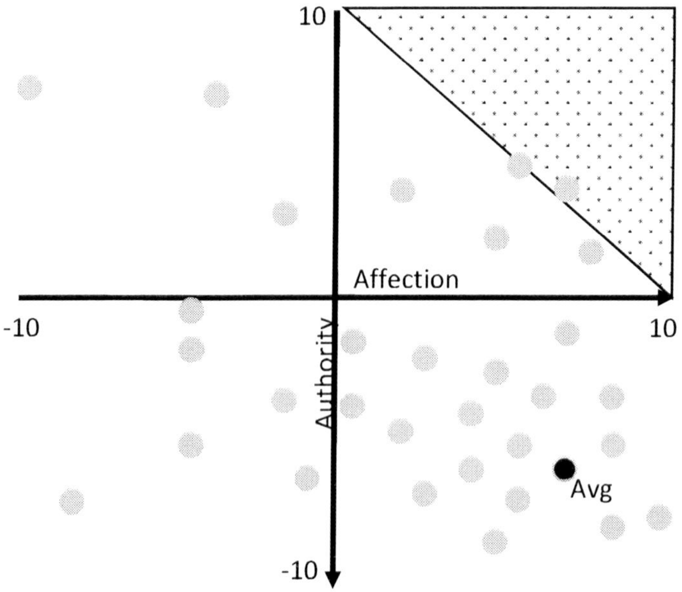

Bridget

- Her friends and family would describe her as ‘adorable’, ‘cute’ or ‘warm’.
- Movie characters or celebrities she is often compared to: Bridget Jones (Bridget Jones’s Diary), Phoebe Bouffuet (Friends), Baby Spice (Spice Girls).

Matt

- His friends and family would describe him as a 'a really nice guy', 'cute' and 'warm'.
- Movie characters or celebrities he is often compared to: Jim Levenstein (American Pie), Joey Tribbiani (Friends), Samwell Tarly (Game of Thrones), Peeta Mellark (Hunger Games), Justin Bieber, Mark Zuckerberg.

Bridget and Matt:

- are too polite and let people have their say.
- put most people on a pedestal.
- excessively nod their heads to let others know they are listening.
- let others interrupt them more than they should.
- speak from the nose or throat.
- compliment others a lot

High Authority—High Affection

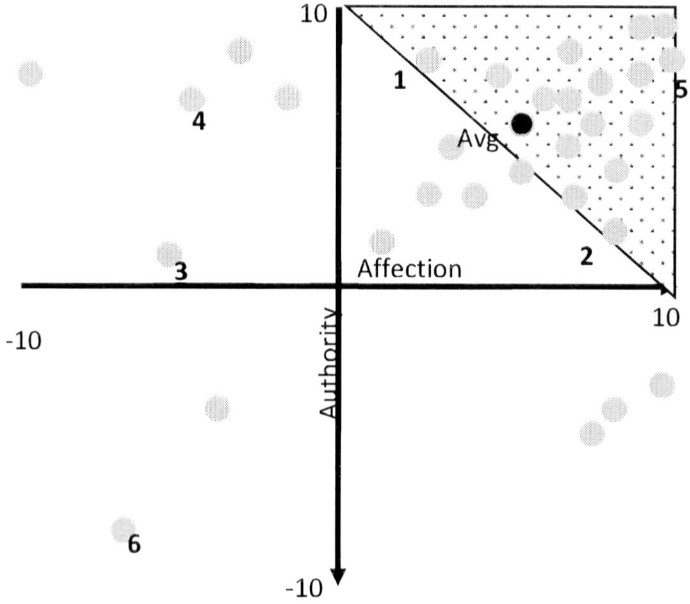

Bella

- Her friends and family would describe her as 'charismatic', 'smart' or 'well-rounded'.
- Movie characters or celebrities she is often compared to: Game of Thrones character Daenerys Targaryan (Before she went mad), Jessica Pearson (Suits), Jennifer Lawrence.

Kush

- His friends and family would describe him as 'charismatic', 'smart' or 'well-rounded'.
- Tyrion Lannister (Game of Thrones), James Bond, Harvey Spectre (Suits), Jonathan Ross, Barack Obama.

Bella and Kush:

- smile a lot.
- make eye contact with everyone.
- consume space
- pause before speaking
- speak at a steady pace with a low tone
- stand still and usher everyone to gather around when a picture is being taken.

Your task over the next 2 weeks is to attend 3 social events where you don't know a single person. In each event, you must play the character of one the above alter egos from beginning to end. Being someone you are not will feel a little awkward at first, but it's really fun after you get into the swing of it! Many of my mentees travel to different parts of the country and visit other universities their friends go to so that they don't bump into anyone they know.

At each event, speak to as many people as possible and pay close attention to how others respond to you. When I attempted to play Steve at a networking event in London, I was pleasantly surprised by the reactions of others. As I tend not to show enough authority in my normal state, forcing myself to be a little arrogant actually balanced me out perfectly.

At another event, I overcompensated and became too cocky. Understandably I split the room in half with people who respected me because they thought I had to be a 'somebody' and those who felt I was unapproachable.

Of course, you can never know for sure what others are thinking but you can get a pretty good idea based on body language and instinct. These experiments show where the boundaries are. Every institution and social circle will have its own set of boundaries that you'll need to adjust to. Taking a few risks and experimenting in this way will help you find where they are each time.

Step 4: Internal Distractions (Day 46 to 67)

All of us suffer from social anxiety every now and then. Unlike other types of anxieties, such as those caused by phobias, social anxiety is much more deeply rooted in our psychology. We can never completely get rid of it so we have to manage it. Some of the tasks that you'll do in this project, such as mindfulness meditation and the 20-Day Rejection Challenge, will help reduce the frequency in which distracting thoughts appear. However, what if you feel anxious or insecure during a critical moment like speaking in public? This is when we can use **A**cknowledge **N**eutralise **T**ransform.

Acknowledge: *'Oh, you again'*

Whenever a negative thought appears, identify and call it out. Often, this is all you need to do to stop thoughts from continuing to distract you.

Neutralise: *'You aren't real'*

Most social anxieties are simply made up simulations by your brain to stop you from falling out with your tribe. Remind yourself that most concerns and fears are pure fiction.

Transform: *'Who cares?'*

Perspective is powerful! Remind yourself of how insignificant your worries are in relation to everything else. You are a mere mortal who has good days and bad days; a human who makes mistakes just like anyone else.

Over the next 3 weeks practice using ANT in your daily life.

Week 1: Focus only on 'Acknowledge'. Every time you catch yourself in an anxious thought, call it out with, 'Oh, you again'.

Thought 1: 'He yawned—am I boring him?'
Thought 2: 'Bore insecurity—*oh, you again'.*

Thought 1: 'I'm not making any sense—she must think I'm an idiot'.
Thought 2: 'Intelligence insecurity—*oh, you again'.*

Thought 1: 'Why am I always nervous, what's wrong with me?'
Thought 2: 'Good old shame—*oh, you again'.*

Week 2: Focus only on 'Acknowledge' and 'Neutralise'. This time use: 'Y*ou aren't real'*

Thought 1: 'He yawned—am I boring him?'
Thought 2: 'Bore insecurity—*oh, you again*'.
Thought 3: 'You aren't real'.

Week 3: Bring all 3 together 'Acknowledge', 'Neutralise' and 'Transform'. This time use '*who cares*?'

Thought 1: 'He yawned—am I boring him?'
Thought 2: 'Bore insecurity—*oh, you again*'.
Thought 3: '*You aren't real'*.
Thought 4: 'w*ho cares?—I could die tomorrow'*.

Thought 1: 'I'm not making any sense—she must think I'm an idiot'.
Thought 2: 'Intelligence insecurity—*oh, you again'*.
Thought 3: '*you aren't real'*.
Thought 4: '*Who cares?—Practice makes perfect and I aced my other interview'*

Step 5: 20 Days of Rejection (Day 68 – 88)

At Yale university in the USA there is a class called 'Mastering Influence and Persuasion' offered by the business school. In one of the course assignments, they get students to practice rejection. One particular student decided to execute the assignment at a top-end five-star hotel in the city.

Dressed in t-shit and jeans, he casually walked through their shiny glass doors and asked the man at the front desk:

"Excuse me sir, do you have any vacancies tonight?"

The lady receptionist confirmed that they did have a few rooms available.

"Great. What's the rate for the cheapest single?"

She responded with an amount around $400.

"Cool," he said. "Could I possibly get the room for free tonight?"

The receptionist looked at him like he was nuts.

He then said, *"I don't have enough money to rent a room, but it would be great if I could stay a night without having to pay for it."*

Front desk lady, unsurprisingly, said that this was against company policy.

He responded, *"Okay, maam, I understand. Could we negotiate some other arrangement? For example, I'm in an acapella group—I'd be happy to sing for your customers in the lobby, in exchange for one night's stay."*

At this point the lady politely told him to get the f*** out, and that's exactly what he did.

The Yale professor based this assignment on the project '100 Days of Rejection' by an entrepreneur named Jia Jiang. After his start-up got turned down by investors, Jiang realised that one of the main roadblocks in his path was his own fear of rejection. To desensitise himself, Jiang spent a hundred days asking for simple, relatively harmless requests that he thought likely to be rejected.

During university, I adapted Jiang's approach and teamed up with a friend. We set each other dares that we had to do every day for a month to help desensitise us from the fear of rejection.

For the next 20 days, I now dare you to:

1. Approach a random girl or guy on public transport and convince them to marry you tonight.

2. Ask a pedestrian to give you a compliment.

3. Convince an estate agent to give you 50% off a property listed in the window.

4. Ask to make your own sandwich at Subway.

5. Convince a waitress or waiter to quit their job.

6. Ask a barista in a coffee shop to put saffron in your latte.

7. Tell staff in Argos that you can't read the catalogue and would rather go round the back and 'have a browse'.

8. Try to buy a book in a library that only lends them out.

9. Get a bus driver to let you have a go.

10. Walk into an almost empty coffee shop and ask anyone sitting down if you can sit where they are.

11. Ask someone on the street for £10.

12. Borrow a random person's mobile phone.

13. Ask a clothing store if you can borrow an item for a few hours.

14. Call a PPI (Payment Protection Insurance) claims company and sell your services to them.

15. Convince the train operator to hold the train for 10 minutes as your friend is running late.

16. Negotiate a 10% discount at a discount or pound store.

17. Go to Toby Carvery and ask to meet Mr Carvery himself.

18. Ask a traffic warden if you can shadow him for a day.

19. Convince your parents to let you drop out and join the army.

20. Order a steak at Nandos.

This is a hilariously fun task which will do wonders for your self-confidence. I did many of these dares after my first graduate interview which went horribly. Soon after I finished the final dare, I went for another interview at a different company which I absolutely aced. This was no coincidence. The dares made me realise how much I live my life in fear of rejection. It was also the first time I realised how harmless most rejections are when you stop being afraid of them. I walked into the second interview with much less fear and buckets of charisma!

This task is probably the most affective out of them all so make sure you complete it fully. At times, every fibre in your body will tell you to run away and doing so might give you an immediate sense of relief, but it won't teach you the important lesson, which is that the things you fear the most about rejection never happen.

Every time you leap you're moving further towards mastering your c-skills. There will be a moment where not jumping becomes more uncomfortable than jumping and that's when you've nailed it!

Step 6: Power Pose (Day 89 – 96)

Hold 3 power poses for two minutes every morning for the next 7 days. This is just to help you remember the poses for when you need to use them in the future. See how you feel during the day, was anything different?

Step 7: Eye Contact (Day 97 – 117)

Out of all the body language guidance I've given you, eye contact is by far the most important. That is why we are dedicating the next 3 weeks on practicing 'extended eye contact'.

1. Notice the eye colour of 35 people you meet this week

2. Maintain eye contact with low-stake strangers

The next time you order an Americano from a barista or a pair of jeans from a clerk, maintain eye contact from the moment you start speaking and don't look away until they've given you a receipt. Even if they are moving around and tapping away on their payment machines, remain focused. Aim to have at least 10 of these interactions during this second week.

3. Talk to everyone by looking directly into their eyes

For the third week, make a proactive effort to look everyone in the eye when you are both speaking and listening. Push to maintain continuous eye contact even after it starts feeling awkward or uncomfortable.

Throughout these 3 weeks, remember that it's impossible for anyone to look into both eyes at the same time, so it's OK to focus on just one eye. Will people notice that you're only looking at one eye and think you're weird? Let's put it this way, do you notice when others are looking at either your left or right eye? Probably not. Others won't notice that you are looking at one eye because they themselves are doing the same. So, don't worry, you won't creep anyone out!

Step 8: Body Language (Day 118 to 138)

For three weeks, use the affirmation 'space invader' to remind you to assume the correct body language. Continuously check yourself throughout the day:

1. Shoulders back and down.
2. Ears in line with shoulders.
3. Pretend a string is attached to the highest point of your head and is being pulled.
4. Smile with wrinkles and teeth showing.
5. Cross your legs when sitting.
6. Move your hands and consume space when speaking.

Step 9: The 'Pause' (Day 139 to 140)

Practice 'the pause' in all your conversations this week. If someone asks you a question or makes a statement expecting a response, wait 2 seconds before speaking. If you're excitable or have a lot of energy you will find this difficult, just remember:

1. There is always time to say what you have to say.
2. You deserve to be heard.
3. Your opinions and views matter.
4. The pause always seems longer in your head than it does to others.

Pausing not only projects charisma and control, it also prevents you from blurting something out that you shouldn't. By the end of this week you'll see a difference in the way others respond to you. People will interrupt you less and listen more.

Step 10: Push/Pull (Day 141 to 147)

Now we get into the conversational techniques! As we discussed in Chapter 26, delivering a compliment to someone creates an awkward and embarrassing tension. Try it today! Deliver a nice comment to someone and watch how they react. Most people will look a little bewildered. There may be an awkward silence followed by them acknowledging it and quickly changing the topic of conversation.

There is nothing wrong with giving someone a compliment or creating this tension. However, letting the tension hang for too long isn't a good idea. Use the push/pull technique—always follow the compliment with a tasteful poke or a question.

Push: Those are really nice shoes.
Pull: Did you get them from Hogwarts?

Remember to smile when you deliver your 'pull'.

Also, keep this technique in mind when receiving a compliment. An individual of high authority doesn't look shocked or embarrassed when complimented. They feel the awkwardness just like everyone else but are quite happy bathing in the tension for a short while before showing appreciation. There is no need to go over and above by thanking them multiple times. Many of my female mentees are guilty of the following:

"Awwww. Thanks so much. It's so nice of you to say that".

A simple 'thanks' with a smile maintains your authority. The other person will subconsciously think, 'This person is used to compliments, they must get a lot'. Following up with a little self-deprecation before moving the conversation will balance your authority with a little affection.

Compliment: I like your shoes.

Response: Thanks (smile), my boyfriend thinks they look like giant lady birds. I like yours too—where did you get them from?

See the counter push/pull? Again, a short comment is all that's needed. You don't need to disprove their compliment using a long-winded explanation:

Response: Thanks (smile), I actually have very bad taste in shoes. I bought these in Primark and needed 2 of my friends to help me because I have no fashion sense whatsoever.

Many Brits have a fear of coming across as arrogant so they continuously devalue themselves when they don't need to. Lean towards authority, especially when giving and receiving compliments.

Step 11: Story Collection (Day 148 to 167)

Write down your top 5 stories that you enjoy telling and that others like hearing. Think of ones that always get a laugh, shock people or draw questions at the end. If you instinctively thought of 1 or 2 just now, stick those on your list immediately. As time goes by, update and add to the list until you have a collection of great personal stories that you can use in any social scenario. Practice these stories in low-stakes scenarios and pay attention to how others react. Remove or replace parts of the story that don't get the reaction you want. I often annotate and highlight parts which always get a laugh or positive reaction. Here's one I used to tell all the time at uni:

"Late one evening, two of my friends and I were walking back from uni to our halls in Kings Cross. From a distance, we heard this loud exhaust noise that was getting closer. ***(pause)***

*We assumed it was a Lamborghini or something so we naturally looked over our shoulders but were left disappointed. It was a black modified VW golf with tinted out windows. It whooshed right past us towards these barriers on the road then suddenly lost control. The car slammed into one of the barriers—****BANG (slap my hands)****—and came to a stop.*

We ran over to see if the driver was OK and as we approached, the car door slowly opened. ***(pause)***

It was an old Caucasian lady. She must have been around 80 years old. Her eyes were really wide open like she was on crack ***(demonstrate)****.*

We looked at each other in disbelief and helped her out. The car was actually in reasonable condition apart from a burst tire so we agreed to fit her spare tire so she could get home. After we were done, she offered us a ride back to halls. It was pretty late at this point so we agreed. The 3 of us got in the back and she started to drive.

*100m down the road, we heard a creak...***(pause)** *then another creak...***(pause)***..and then* **BANG (slap my hands)**.

The tire we fitted popped off, the car tilted back and we started grinding along the road. Sparks flying everywhere! The old lady went crazy! She stopped the car and we got out.

*At this point, we had to call the RAC. I had a 9am lecture and graded exam the next day, so my mates agreed to stay with her and sort everything out while I went home to revise. As I was walking back, a police car stopped right next to me. They rolled down the window and asked me what I was doing. Someone had reported the incident to them and they thought I looked suspicious. I looked at them and said..***(pause)**..

I'm walking home but there are 2 guys harassing an old lady round the corner."

My mates were grilled for about half an hour because the police didn't believe the story or why 2 Asian guys were with an old 80-year-old lady and a banged up Golf at midnight on a Tuesday evening! The look on their faces when they came home was priceless. They got me back eventually.

This was the longest story I had in my collection. It took me a couple minutes to recite, but it never failed to hold people's attention even in large groups or noisy environments. Also, the ending of the story always got a laugh followed by the question, 'What happened to your mates?'.

Why was the story so effective? First of all, unlike others in my collection, it's very PG 13 so I could tell it to anyone. Secondly, there were lots of twists and turns which kept people wanting more. Finally, because it actually happened, it was easy to get lost in the story and describe all the small details. Try to ensure your stories have these characteristics as well.

As I told the story to more people, I noticed parts where people were dozing off or losing focus. You can always tell because they look away or react later than expected. It's at those moments where I bang my hands together to wake them up or increase my volume and expand my body language. Later at home, I'd annotate the story in my collection to remind me.

It might seem extreme, strange or even unnatural to approach your social life in such a structured and almost academic way. However, these are the extremes I initially went to gain a social edge. I know for a fact that others, including the most charismatic and successful people I know, went to similar lengths. Over time, through practice, you will deliver your stories in a charismatic way and writing them down will no longer be necessary.

Dedicate the next two weeks to practicing your top 5 stories on people you've never met before. Keep an eye on their body language and reactions as you speak. They will give you clues as to where the weak parts are then make those changes in your collection. Through trial and error, you will optimise your stories to create a positive impact that people will remember you for.

Step 12: Grujems (Day 168 to 177)

Your final task in the program is a fun one! Learn and use at least one of each Grujem over the next 9 days. Feel free to use your own or mine:

Games: Fives, Frog, Going to the moon, Never have I ever and Heads up.

Riddles: Short man in a lift and splitting £25.

Jokes: Millennial moth and orange head.

Magic: Illuminati and 3-card Diamond Monte.

The Charisma Project

Step	Day	Task	Summary
1	1-14	Measure your c-skills	Myers Briggs, feedback forms, low & high-stake interviews
2	15-30	Presence	'Every person is an opportunity', mindfulness & Eyelash Snap
3	31-45	Authority & affection	Tara/Steve, Bridgett/Matt & Bella/Kush
4	46-67	Internal distractions	'Oh, you again'-'You aren't real'-'You could die tomorrow'
5	68-88	20 days of rejection	I dare you to…
6	89-96	Power-Pose	3 power-poses for two minutes every morning
7	97-117	Eye contact	What colour are their eyes?
8	118-138	Body language	'Spatially greedy'
9	139-140	The 'Pause'	Pause for 2 seconds before responding
10	141-147	Push/Pull	Nice shoes. Did you get them from Hogwarts?

11	148-167	Story collection	Find your top 5 stories and tell them to everyone
12	168-177	Grujems	Games, riddles, jokes & magic

Chapter 34
Onwards & Upwards

"People just gravitate towards you. How do you do that?"

This is what a rival candidate said to me after we both finished a second-round assessment centre at a top asset manager in the city. As I thought about the past few months and all the crazy extreme things I did to become more charismatic, it dawned on me that no one had ever said anything like that to me before. Without even thinking, I reactively said:

"Proactive practice".

Most assume that charisma or people skills cannot be taught or learned. However, they really are just like everything else. If you focus on learning the theory and practicing in real life, you'll improve. I'm a living, breathing proof of that.

The best part is that you don't need to go out of your way to practice. Unless you live in Antarctica you'll interact with hundreds of people each week. Each conversation is not only an opportunity to develop a relationship but also an opportunity to practice. Even to this day, before picking up a ringing phone or entering the door of a birthday party, I pause for a moment and think:

'You're not Jimmy'.

or

'Gorilla'

or

'Eyes'

or

'Pause'

I'll use some affirmation to compose myself and move into a charismatic state. All the techniques come rushing back and autopilot switches on. There is no better feeling than when you clear out the cobweb of social anxiety to allow your true personality to shine. There is nothing more satisfying than confidently commanding the room and leaving a conversation or party knowing you were at the top of your game.

By committing to and executing the 6-Month Charisma Project you will be able to achieve this. A lifelong commitment to mastering your c-skills will transform your personal and professional life.

It's time to stop living in fear of rejection, humiliation and embarrassment, to stop letting your anxieties control you. Imagine how much better your life would be if you had never turned down a date or social event because you were anxious, if you had never bombed an interview because you didn't know what to say, and if you had taken every opportunity you've ever had with open arms.

It's not too late to make a change and to make sure that the regrets you have now don't evolve into bigger regrets in the future. Just follow the guidelines in this book and your life will change for the better!

Good luck on your journey!

FAQ

I need more help. How do I contact you?

Whether you need help managing social anxiety, interviews, executing the Charisma Project or anything else; contact us on www.AcademicUnderdogs.com. We'll be happy to help!

We also offer mentorship programmes to help you succeed at university and beyond. Previous mentees have gone onto achieve top grades and built the confidence to impress in interviews. Using our network of employers, many of them have also been placed at fast growing start-ups around the world.

We do everything in our power to ensure you leave university with your head held high and hit the ground running as a graduate.

Do you have any other books?

Yes! *How to be Admired & Respected* is book 2 of 3 in the *Level Up* series. Book 1, *How to ACE Your Degree*, shows you how to achieve top grades at university. Book 3, *How to Land Your Dream Graduate Job,* contains a 4-step plan to help you find and secure a career that's right for you.

How to ACE Your Degree

How to Land Your Dream Graduate Job

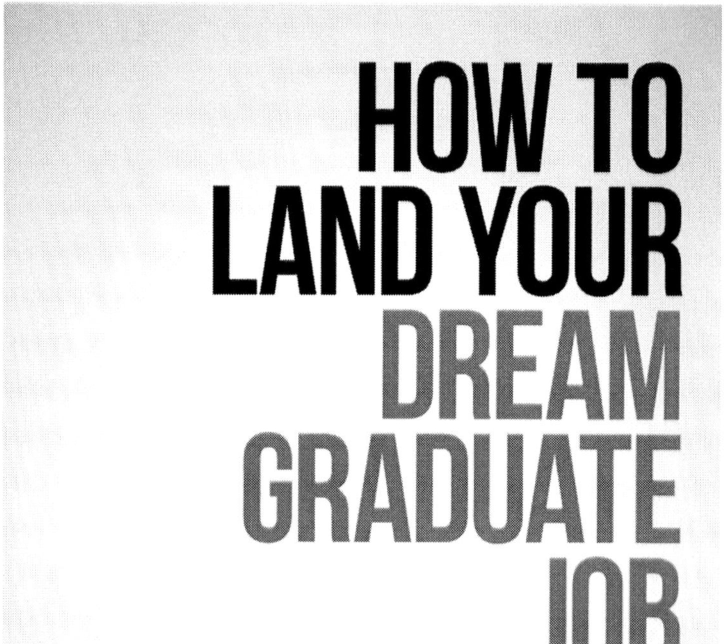